BALANCED LIVING
ON A
TIGHTROPE

BALANCED LIVING
ON A
TIGHTROPE

TERRY POWELL

VICTOR BOOKS®

A DIVISION OF SCRIPTURE PRESS PUBLICATIONS INC.
USA CANADA ENGLAND

Unless otherwise noted, Scripture quotations in this book are from
the *New American Standard Bible*, © The Lockman Foundation
1960, 1962, 1963, 1968, 1971, 1972, 1973, 1975, 1977. Quotations marked TLB are taken from *The Living Bible*, © 1971, Tyndale House Publishers, Wheaton, IL 60189. Used by permission.
Quotations marked NIV are from the *Holy Bible, New International
Version*, © 1973, 1978, 1984, International Bible Society. Used by
permission of Zondervan Bible Publishers. Quotations marked PH
are from J.B. Phillips: *The New Testament in Modern English*, Re-
vised Edition, © J.B. Phillips, 1958, 1960, 1972, permission of
Macmillan Publishing Co. and Collins Publishers.

Library of Congress Cataloging-in-Publication Data

Powell, Terry.
 Balanced living on a tightrope / by Terry Powell.
  p.   cm.
 Includes bibliographical references.
 ISBN 0-89693-145-5
 1. Bible. O.T. Proverbs—Meditations. 2. Christian life—Biblical teaching.   I. Title.
 BS1465.4.P68   1990
 223'.706—dc20
                              90-15531
                                CIP

1   2   3   4   5   6   7   8   9   10   Printing/Year   95   94   93   92   91

TABLE OF CONTENTS

DEDICATION

This book is affectionately dedicated to John Mark Powell, the provider of comic relief in our daily grind.

May the keys to spiritual riches offered in Proverbs mean as much to Mark as the keys to our family car.

CHAPTER ONE

Gaining God's Perspectives

.Picture yourself as a parent of a college girl. She has two problems common among students: low grades and no money. She needs to break the news of both to you, but she figures you'll blow your top and have trouble understanding. What strategy will she employ?

Charles Swindoll tells about a coed in precisely this situation. She used a creative approach to soften the blows of reality. Here's the letter to her parents, followed by Swindoll's comments:

Dear Mom and Dad,

Just thought I'd drop you a note to clue you in on my plans. I've fallen in love with a guy named Jim. He quit high school after grade eleven to get married. About a year ago he got a divorce.

We've been going steady for two months and plan to get married in the fall. Until then, I've decided to move into his apartment (I think I might be pregnant).

At any rate, I dropped out of school last week, although I'd like to finish college sometime in the future.

On the next page she continued:

> *Mom and Dad, I just want you to know that everything I've written so far in this letter is false. NONE of it is true.*
> *But Mom and Dad, it IS true that I got a C in French and flunked Math. It IS true that I'm going to need some more money for my tuition payments.*

Pretty sharp sharp coed! Even bad news can sound like good news if it is seen from a certain vantage point. So much in life depends on "where you're coming from" as you face your circumstances. The secret, of course, is perspective.[1]

Perspectives from Proverbs
Perspective. Just as the coed used this concept to her advantage, so can you. According to *Webster's New Collegiate Dictionary*, perspective is "the capacity to view things in their true relations or relative importance." Put simply, perspective is the ability to see issues clearly, to distinguish the temporary from the eternal, the important from the trivial. The coed knew that poor grades and an empty pocketbook were minor matters compared to the fictional circumstances described on page 1 of her letter.

Whether or not we cultivate an accurate perspective on life depends on who shapes our attitudes and values. Who prescribes the lenses we look through when we view other people and activities that go on around us? What's the source of the assumptions and convictions which forge our behavior from day to day?

If we accept the label *Christian*, then God should prescribe those lenses. How we view things—and ultimately, how we act—should square with *His* perceptions. And the lens which gives us God's viewpoint is the Bible. If Christians fail to see life experiences through the perspective lens of Scripture, we'll find ourselves marching along after the dinosaurs to an inglorious extinction.

That's the reason for this paperback on the book of Proverbs. I hope to disclose God's perspectives on everyday things like the money you make and your relationships in the home. Who doesn't need to tap into God's wisdom and see issues from a heavenly vantage point? His opinion is more reliable than any syndicated advice columnist or talk show guest you can name.

In *You and Your Network*, Fred Smith said, "We seldom are intense about learning anything which we are not going to use very shortly."² Bank on it: the material we explore in Proverbs will be usable the day you read it! Studying this ancient book is like getting a Ph.D. in living. Its content is as up-to-date as the latest issue of *USA Today* newspaper. The following questions provide a sampling of the subjects discussed in Proverbs. They'll prove that I'm not trying to dump obsolete material on you.

● What are the consequences of self-indulgence?

● How can I avoid moral erosion in an X-rated culture?

● What effect do the people I'm around have on my character?

● How should I respond when I'm criticized?

● When I'm pressed to make decisions about job changes, or parenting choices, what guidelines can help me?

● What does the Bible mean when it tells me to "fear the Lord"? Am I supposed to cringe in His presence?

● Why is pride considered "Public Enemy #1" for the Christian?

● What's the best way to use and invest my money?

● What is a "godly" woman like?

● In what specific ways does the tongue get people in trouble? How can I control mine?

● What are some tips for getting along with problem people? For confronting people when they need it?

A Christian chemistry professor at a large university told his students, "Christianity is not a lecture. It is a laboratory science." Bull's-eye! We confirm our faith in Christ not by passing a theology quiz but through daily experimentation. And the laboratory is the office where you work, not just the Sunday

School classroom; a traffic jam on the freeway, not just a summer Bible conference. Tackling the topics in Proverbs will help you exercise your faith, not just cram more biblical data into the creases of your mind.

But before we delve into those topics, let me formally introduce you to the Old Testament Book of Proverbs.

Transistorized Truth
To familiarize you with the nature of Proverbs, I turn to a parable Calvin Miller tells in *The Taste of Joy*. The story centers on a king who ordered his wise men to condense all human wisdom into as few words as possible:

> They returned after twelve years of work with twelve thick volumes. "It is too large," protested the king. "Condense it further!" So the wise men returned in a year and presented one large volume in place of the twelve. "It's still too large," protested the king. They went out again, only to return the following day with a single statement written on a slip of paper—all the world's wisdom in one line: *There is no free lunch.*[3]

In Proverbs, you can get the scoop on God's perspectives without having to plow through a textbook in theology. Like a transistor radio that fits in a shirt pocket, the sayings in Proverbs are spiritual transistors that can readily be stored in your heart. Author Haydn Gilmore calls the maxims in Proverbs "transistorized" truth because they present wisdom in the smallest possible package.[4]

Most books of the Bible are written either as a narrative, which tells a story, or as a letter, teeming with advice from a leader to a group of believers. Not Proverbs. It is a thirty-one chapter catalog of short, pithy remarks on everything from keeping a lid on your temper to the side effects of drinking too much booze. Unlike the content in most books of the Bible, a verse you're reading in Proverbs may cover an entirely different topic than the verse that precedes or follow it.

Our English term for *proverb* stems from two Latin words which mean "instead of words." So a *proverb* is a sentence of condensed wisdom that's offered in the place of a whole spate of words. The writers cut a swath through excess verbiage by summarizing a general principle of life with a particular illustration. For instance, ponder Proverbs 11:22: "As a ring of gold in a swine's snout, so is a beautiful woman who lacks discretion." Not even a book-length manuscript could drive home the point better: *poor character spoils a woman's physical attractiveness.*

Scholars credit King Solomon with the proverbs in chapters 1–24 of the collection. Around 950 years before Christ, he either wrote or compiled these bits of advice. What we read in chapters 25–31 is divinely sanctioned wisdom from other sources. In the first nine chapters of Proverbs, Solomon salutes the value of wisdom, and tells how to get it. The remaining chapters apply wisdom to a wide range of relational contacts and circumstances. In fact, the authors mention over 180 different types of people in Proverbs. That should encompass every type of character you run into at church or in the market place.

Interpreting Proverbs

What's the long-range goal of the paperback you're holding? To give you a taste of the smorgasbord of truth in Proverbs so that you'll make this taken-for-granted part of Scripture a staple item in your spiritual diet. Long after this book is out of print, Proverbs will offer you fresh menus from which to choose.

Before you start sampling the morsels God dishes up in this Bible book, it's important to understand the type of literature it represents. Otherwise, it's easy to wrench the wrong meaning out of a verse. To get its messages across, Proverbs employs poetic language, including numerous figures of speech. Charles Sell describes the nature of a proverb this way:

When a colleague of mine and I were teaching a class together, he created a proverb of his own to explain their nature. Waiting for class to begin, he was outside prancing around in an evening drizzle. Glancing down at his shoes, he said, "Aha, I've got it." Smiling before the class, he later gave his example: "Walk in the mud and your shoes will get muddy." He explained. First, a proverb is a brief statement. It packs more of a wallop that way and is more easily memorized. My colleague could have expressed his idea about muddy shoes another way: "Whenever a person commits an act or presents himself to a set of circumstances that is unseemly or in any way tainted with immorality and ungodliness, that person will in some way, no matter how slight, be affected by that influence." This long sentence lulls you to sleep, while the first one about muddy shoes jars you awake.

When my fellow teacher spoke of mud, everyone knew he wasn't giving a lesson about clean shoes. He was warning us to stay away from pornography, drugs, bad company, and other negative influences. That's the genius of a proverb: it makes an obvious statement to get across a not-so-obvious truth.[5]

We can't interpret comments in Proverbs in the same way as we interpret statements of fact, such as, "It's snowing outside," or "We become Christians by trusting in Christ." Instead, we must extract the general message or broad principle from a proverb without turning its particular remark into a rigid absolute. Once again, let's learn from Charles Sell about this sticky issue of interpretation:

The Hebrews tended to make general statements without worrying about the exceptions, appealing to the reader's common sense to see this. For example, Proverbs 16:3 assures success to those who first commit their plans to God. But committing alone does not guarantee prosperity; many persons trust God to help them fulfill foolish goals. The proverb is not true for them.

Because they are principles, we must also not turn all of them into promises from God. God is using the wise writers of the proverbs to describe what usually occurs in life. For example, one proverb states, "When a man's ways are pleasing to the Lord, He makes even his enemies live at peace with him" (16:7). The principle here is that being rightly related to God will keep you rightly related to others. God doesn't guarantee this will always happen. Jesus was without sin, yet He was murdered by His enemies.[6]

When interpreting Proverbs, we must also be careful to avoid taking figures of speech literally. When you come across Proverbs 6:29, you'll read that a man who *touches* another man's wife will be punished. Does that mean you'll go to jail for accidently bumping into another man's spouse in the ticket line at the theater? Obviously not. The word *touch* in this verse is a nice way of talking about having sex with her. Or consider the way Proverbs 15:25 exaggerates in order to get a point across: "The Lord will tear down the house of the proud, but He will establish the boundary of the widow." That's called a hyperbole: a figure of speech which overstates a matter in order to convey a message. The author isn't promising that the minute you feel proud of your remodeled kitchen, its walls will collapse. But he is saying that God resists the proud and defends the helpless.

I could drone on about the different literary forms in Proverbs, but I don't want your eyelids to get stuck at half-mast during this opening chapter.

Treasure Hunt

I have already quoted from Charles Sell's fine book, A *House On The Rock*, but allow me to share with you one additional piece of information I gleaned from his volume. It's a true story about lost treasure at sea. In 1985, deep-sea divers located the treasure of the sunken Spanish galleon *Nuestra Senora de Atocha*. Mel Fisher and his crew hauled to the surface $400 million worth of gold and silver bars and emeralds by the quart. Experts estimated the total value of the salvage at $4 billion!

We envy this fortune hunter until we discover the price he paid for the search. Mel Fisher had been crisscrossing the sea for fifteen frustrating years looking for that sunken ship, at a cost of $70 million. Some crew members went without pay for six years. And here's a more sobering fact: The treasure hunt cost Mel Fisher the lives of his son and daughter-in-law. When their hunting vessel capsized in a storm, they drowned.[7]

Are we as committed to salvaging the precious cargo of Proverbs? God doesn't drop His gems of insight into our laps without any work on our part. We won't pay as steep a price as Mel Fisher, yet claiming the fortune in Proverbs will cost some time and effort.

If you honestly want God's perspectives on the things that matter most to you, read the following chapters in this paperback. Then make a treasure hunt through Proverbs a lifetime hobby. "If you seek her [wisdom] as silver, and search for her as hidden treasures; *then* you will discern the fear of the Lord, and discover the knowledge of God" (Prov. 2:4-5).

Here's a reading schedule to guide you in your hunt through Proverbs. Digest a chapter a day, corresponding to the day of the month. If it's April 5, read Proverbs 5, and so on. When you miss a day, don't fret over making up the previous chapter. You can make it up the following month, when you read through the Book of Proverbs again. Such repeated exposure is the only way God's wisdom can nuzzle its way into your mind and heart.

Digest the teachings in Proverbs, and when *your* daughter or son sends bad news from college, you'll know how to respond.

CHAPTER TWO
Finishing What We Start

Recently I celebrated (is that the right word?) my fortieth birthday. My wife invited a few friends over. They gift wrapped heartwarming presents such as Geritol, denture cleanser, and laxatives. When I proudly announced that I felt younger than ever after losing thirty pounds, a former pal said, "I figured you were on a diet. Even your hair looks thinner!"

Now that I have the credibility to write on the subject, I determined it is my duty to make you aware of all the telltale signs of growing older. Those of us over forty may not get the same kick out of the following indicators as you younger whippersnappers. But at least our medicine cabinets are well-stocked.

You know you're growing old . . .

- when you feel like the night before and you haven't been anywhere.
- when your little black book contains only names ending in M.D.
- when you know all the answers, but nobody asks you the questions.
- when you look forward to a dull evening at home.
- when you sit in a rocking chair and can't make it go.

- when your knees buckle and your belt won't.
- when dialing long distance wears you out.
- when your back goes out more than you do.
- when you sink your teeth into a steak and they stay there.
- when you turn out the light for economic reasons rather than romantic ones.
- when you step out of the shower, and you're glad the mirror is all fogged up.
- when you lean over to pick up something off the floor, and you start wondering, *Now what else can I do while I'm down here?*

I don't know about you, but I want to die *young*—as late as possible!

Most folks grow wiser as they grow older. It's generally accepted that old age and wisdom go hand-in-glove. Decades of experiencing ups and downs usually result in old-fashioned common sense. (The unfortunate part is this: by the time we learn how to make the most of life, most of it is gone!)

But there are exceptions to the "older is wiser" rule. Ironically, perhaps the most famous exception started out as the world's wisest man. Since we were knee-high to a gnat, we've heard accolades about Solomon's distinguished discernment. His name is synonymous with the word *wisdom*. Yet the older he got, the more foolishly he acted. With every new wrinkle, he became a more absurd demonstration of reckless living.

Don't get me wrong. The proverbs he wrote are right on target. But as the years progressed, he failed to practice what he preached. Though a wealth of insight filled his head, his heart gradually became poverty-stricken.

Solomon's Success

When Solomon was just 15 years old, a royal limousine shuttled him from a Middle School classroom to the throne of Israel. A quick glance at the scrapbook clippings summarizing his forty-year reign reveals a public relations dream come true. Solomon's reign launched an era of peace and prosperity for Israel. Solomon's early popularity eclipsed that of his father King David.

His list of achievements reads like a page out of *Who's Who*. He wrote at least 3,000 proverbs and 1,005 songs. He unveiled a college-level grasp of botany, zoology, horticulture, architecture, philosophy, and literature. As a result of his diplomacy, Israel's borders expanded to their greatest geographical extent. Residents of nearby nations shook in their sandals at the size of his military stockpile. To top it all off, he was wealthier than any wizard on Wall Street. His personal residence was so lavish that it would make a Beverly Hills mansion look like a crude shanty in an inner-city ghetto. When he wanted a sip of Maxwell House or a Diet Coke, he sipped the beverage from solid gold drinking vessels.

What accounts for his political savvy and bulging bank account? Here's the reason he succeeded: "And the Lord his God was with him and exalted him greatly" (2 Chron. 1:1). God was his Secretary of State, Chief of Staff, Public Relations expert, and investment broker all rolled into one. God prospered him because, as an adolescent ruler, Solomon revealed a spiritual sensitivity.

His inauguration was still front-page news when he begged God for the wisdom needed to fulfill his job description: "Give Thy servant an understanding heart to judge Thy people to discern between good and evil. For who is able to judge this great people of Thine?" (1 Kings 3:9) Solomon's humility impressed God so much that He threw in material prosperity as a bonus: "I have done according to your words. Behold, I have given you a wise and discerning heart, so that there has been no one like you before you, nor shall one like you arise after you. And I have also given you what you have not asked, both riches and honor" (1 Kings 3:12-13). It's clear that as a young man, Solomon followed his own advice about relying on God: "Trust in the Lord with all your heart, and do not lean on your own understanding" (Prov. 3:5).

Because the Lord pushed all the right buttons, "Solomon's wisdom surpassed the wisdom of all the sons of the east and all the wisdom of Egypt . . . and his fame was known in all the surrounding nations" (1 Kings 4:30-31). One of his most important executive decisions was the construction of an ornate worship facility. When workers completed the temple, Solomon led thousands of Jews in prayer at a formal dedication service. His prayer scraped the Milky Way with its elegance. God showed His approval of Solomon's prayer by zapping a burnt offering with a fireball from heaven. Even movie moguls such as George Lucas and Stephen Speilberg would have been proud of the special effects!

Before you start drooling over Solomon's advantages, though, remember this: he ran out of gas before reaching the finish line. The perks of power derailed his commitment to God. He became too earthly minded to be of any heavenly good. Intoxicated by one too many gulps of worldly pleasure, he started living life according to his own script, instead of God's. Disobedience diluted his character, and his commitment to God receded at a faster clip than his hairline.

Crafty Compromise

According to *Webster's New Collegiate Dictionary*, one of the meanings of the word *compromise* is: "to make a shameful or disreputable concession." Compromise is making a choice based on personal rewards at the expense of ethical convictions. To put it in contemporary terms, compromise is carrying ink pens home from the office despite a deep-rooted conviction against stealing. Or renting an R-rated movie despite an awareness that its characters play fast and loose with sex.

Compromise with God's Word revealed termites in the timber of Solomon's character. One minute he'd pray zealously to the Lord. The next minute he'd make a decision that left God with the short end of the stick. For an example of his inconsistent allegiance, turn to 1 Kings 3:1. He took a step of political expediency when he "formed a marriage alliance with Pharaoh King of Egypt, and took Pharaoh's daughter and brought her to the city of David." The royal wedding served as a peace treaty with Egypt. Yet Solomon knew God had forbidden Jews to marry folks from foreign countries. Before the Israelites ever entered the Promised Land, God had said concerning their relationship with other races, "You shall not intermarry with them" (Deut. 7:3). He would later discover that the price he paid for peace was inflationary.

Another example of Solomon's sacrificing conviction at the altar of convenience is found in 1 Kings 3:3: "Solomon loved the Lord, walking in the statutes of his father David, *except he sacrificed and burned incense on the high places*" (emphasis mine). The "high places" referred to altars erected for the worship of idols. To pacify people around him who clung to the false gods of the Canaanites, Solomon protected their worship centers. He knew their gods didn't exist, yet he even participated in the pagan worship services just to keep the people on his side. His refusal to wipe out the pagan altars defied a previous command handed down by Moses: "You shall tear down their altars, and smash their sacred pillars" (Deut. 7:5). The true God was jealous of the attention paid to man-made idols.

How would God feel if Billy Graham joined Muslims in a pilgrimage to Mecca, and in a prayer to Allah, just to improve his image in the Middle East? Of course, Graham wouldn't make such a concession. Yet that's the kind of fence-straddling faith Solomon had. He feared the opinion of men more than the consequences of sin. He failed to heed the advice he had given others about righteousness: "The integrity of the upright will guide them, but the falseness of the treacherous will destroy them" (Prov. 11:3).

First Kings 11:6 says that the seed of compromise sprouted from the shallow soil of his half-hearted commitment to God: Solomon "did not follow the Lord *fully*." Almost 3,000 years have passed, yet such fickle fidelity toward the Lord is still as commonplace as a sore throat in January. Like Solomon, too many of us serve the Lord in such a way as to avoid offending the devil.

Anthony Munoz didn't mind putting a body block on Satan, though. He's a perennial All-Pro offensive lineman for the Cin-

cinnati Bengals. He played in the 1989 Super Bowl. Prior to the start of the 1986 season, *Playboy* magazine wanted to interview Munoz for a major sports story about key "match-ups" between offensive and defensive players in the NFL. Enter the temptation for this Christian athlete to compromise. "This was a story about the best guys in the league, which made it an honor of sorts to be singled out," explained Munoz. "*Playboy* wanted to fly me out for a day of interviews and pics."

But the readers of *Playboy's* "Pigskin Preview" that summer didn't find the bulging blocker splashed between the indecent photos of the opposite sex. After praying and consulting with his pastor, Munoz turned down the interview. He declined the offer because the magazine isn't compatible with his moral beliefs. More important than pumping up his athletic image was exercising his convictions. "With my beliefs as a Christian, I couldn't see myself doing it," said Munoz.[1]

Munoz avoided the "domino effect" of a single act of compromise. Just as you can topple a whole row of dominoes with a slight shove on the first one, you can start a chain reaction of destructive choices with one instance of rationalization. One decision to chuck your values makes it that much easier to do the same another time.

Solomon "loved the Lord, *except . . .* " Is there an "except clause" in *your* devotion to God?

Giving in to Greed
You already know that God granted Solomon's request for wisdom. And on top of that, the Lord made an eye-popping deposit in Solomon's bank account. He threw in riches as a bonus because Solomon had made an unselfish, humble request. So the king's possessions didn't pose a spiritual problem — until his possessions pulled a political coup and stole God's place on the throne of Solomon's heart. Before he knew it, Solomon developed a thirst for things that couldn't be quenched.

Stuff this point into the creases of your mind: *having lots of things wasn't Solomon's vice. His problem was a craving for more things.* Greed caused dissatisfaction with God's gifts, and injected the poison of a "more" mentality within Solomon's bloodstream. Before the first king was ever crowned in Israel, God had warned future rulers about the energy-sapping pull of greed. He had left explicit instructions for each king to read: "He shall not multiply horses for himself . . . nor shall he greatly increase silver and gold for himself" (Deut. 17:16-17). Perhaps God dropped wealth in Solomon's lap early in his reign so the king wouldn't have to worry about the next meal, or the threat of the palace electricity being turned off. Since Solomon had plenty, he could focus his attention on governing the people. Yet Solomon didn't cooperate with God's intentions. He spent as much time and energy managing his money as he did serving the country.

A tip-off to Solomon's love for luxury was the time it took to build his personal palace. The temple he built for God was finished in seven years. Construction of his own residence took thirteen years! His expensive tastes resulted in crippling taxation of his subjects. By importing slave labor, he saved big bucks on construction projects. In a business transaction with King Hiram of Tyre, Solomon traded several cities in Galilee for building supplies. When it came time for Hiram to claim the cities, their skyline didn't impress him. He felt jilted in the trade-off. There's no record of Solomon ever trying to make things right. When greed reigns, the conscience goes into rigor mortis. We start valuing things more than people. The irony is that Solomon himself warned folks about putting things above relationships: "Better is a little with fear of the Lord, than great treasure and turmoil with it. Better is a dish of vegtables where love is, than a fattened ox and hatred with it" (Prov. 15:16-17).

Chris Zwingelberg explains how an uncontrolled appetite for things often leads to a tragic conclusion.

Radio personality Paul Harvey tells the story of how an Eskimo kills a wolf. The account is grisly, yet it offers fresh insight into the consuming, self-destructive nature of sin.

First the Eskimo coats his knife blade with animal blood

and allows it to freeze. Then he adds another layer of blood, and another, until the blade is completely concealed by frozen blood.

Next, the hunter fixes his knife in the ground with the blade up. When a wolf follows his sensitive nose to the source of the scent and discovers the bait he licks it, tasting the fresh-frozen blood. He begins to lick faster, more and more vigorously, lapping the blade until the keen edge is bare. Feverishly now, harder and harder the wolf licks the blade in the Arctic night. So great becomes his craving for blood that the wolf does not notice the razor sharp sting of the naked blade on his tongue nor does he recognize the instant at which his insatiable thirst is being satisfied by his *own* warm blood. His carnivorous appetite just craves more—until the dawn finds him dead in the snow![2]

Unless we put a rein on our craving for things, it will consume our appetite for God. As an old man, looking back on his lavish lifestyle, the sharp blade of regret slashed Solomon's conscience. Writing in his journal, he first acknowledged his material bent: "I built houses for myself. . . . I collected for myself silver and gold. . . . All that my eyes desired I did not refuse them" (Ecc. 2:4, 8, 10). Did lucrative investments satisfy his soul? Just the opposite. He concluded: "All was vanity and striving after wind and there was no profit under the sun" (Ecc. 2:11). A hollow human heart bleeds more than a wolf carcass lying in the arctic snow.

Solomon forgot that there are two ways to get rich: one is to have all you want, and the other is to be satisfied with what you have. If things like BMW's and a luxurious house become the basis for our self-esteem, we'll never own enough to feel good about ourselves.

Seduced By Sex

Little by little Solomon's character decayed. To the erosive sins of compromise and materialism, he added an addiction to sex. In the personal journal referred to earlier, he also confessed, "I provided for myself . . . the pleasures of men—many concubines" (Ecc. 2:8).

That was the understatement of the millennium! According to 1 Kings 11:3, he had "seven hundred wives, princesses, and three hundred concubines." When he wasn't huddling with his banker, he was hopping in bed with someone he hardly knew. The wives and concubines had to take a number just to get a date with him. Solomon slept around despite a divine directive for sexual purity. In the same breath in which Moses warned future kings about materialism, he said, "Neither shall he multiply wives for himself, lest his heart turn away" (Deut. 17:17).

What was the effect of lust on Solomon? His harem drained him of affection for God. The wives from non-Jewish backgrounds diverted his attention away from Jehovah to their idols. They "turned his heart away after other gods" (1 Kings 11:4). Perhaps John was meditating on Solomon when he wrote, "If anyone loves the world, the love of the Father is not in him" (1 John 2:15). Solomon didn't worry about catching AIDS, yet his X-rated lifestyle infected his heart, immunizing him to the truth of God's Word.

Solomon would nod in agreement with David Morley's observation: "The sex drive is so intense that it can cut across all lines of judgment and intelligence. It can make a man cheat, steal, or kill, or make him throw away all his wealth or talent in order to pursue it."[3]

It's easier to yield to sexual temptation when we start believing that the benefits outweigh the negative consequences. Erwin Lutzer describes the deception of this mind-set:

> Samuel Baker tells a story of Egyptian troops who were dying of thirst in the Nubian Desert. In the distance they saw what they thought was water, but the Arabian guide warned them that it was only a mirage. An argument erupted and the guide was killed. The whole regiment rushed toward the water. Mile after mile the thirsty troops

trudged deeper into the desert as the glistening mirage led them on. Finally they realized that the lake they thought was there was burning sand. They died pursuing something that wasn't even there. A search party discovered their withered corpses.[4]

Sensuality was a mirage for Solomon. He thought it would satisfy a thirst for pleasure. Instead, the heat of his passion resulted in a barren, parched heart. His later years were spent harvesting the wild oats that he sowed. Yet Solomon knew better. He was addressing the issue of sexual promiscuity when he wrote, "Can a man take fire in his bosom, and his clothes not be burned? Or can a man walk on hot coals, and his feet not be scorched?" (Prov. 6:27-28)

Divine Discipline

Solomon's all-you-can-eat buffet lifestyle eventually led to heartburn. Except it was the kind of pain he couldn't cure with a dose of Pepto-Bismol. His brazen defiance was an invitation for the Lord to discipline him. Scripture makes it clear that God didn't ignore the severity of Solomon's sins. Once again, he painfully experienced the truth of his own words: "The deeds of a man's hands will return to him" (Prov. 12:14). Consequences came in the following forms:

● *God's anger.* For a long time God exercised patience with Solomon's inconsistency. But when he dabbled in idolatry to pacify his foreign wives, that was the last straw! "Now the Lord was angry with Solomon because his heart was turned away from the Lord, the God of Israel who . . . had commanded him concerning this thing, that he should not go after other gods; but he did not observe what the Lord had commanded" (1 Kings 11:9-10).

The Bible makes it crystal clear that God is slow to anger and forgiving. But His unconditional love shouldn't lull us into believing that He's soft and tolerant toward sin. His concern for us is what drives Him to discipline us. He isn't above permitting pain in our lives as an attention-getting device. One type of psychological pain Solomon experienced was broken fellowship with his Creator.

• *Civil rebellion.* One of the judgments stemming from God's anger was a split kingdom. Solomon had worked long and hard for a united empire. One of his long-term goals was to eliminate internal factions as well as foreign enemies. Yet God's ax fell on the king's burden for unity. "Because you have not kept My covenant and My statutes . . . I will surely tear the kingdom from you," God promised (1 Kings 11:11). Not long after that, Jeroboam—one of Solomon's most trusted warriors— rebelled against the king. Though the nation didn't split until Solomon died, God informed Solomon in advance that his dream of unity would be crushed. Even before he died, civil unrest began unraveling Solomon's reign. Sure enough—Solomon's heir was left with only one tribe of Jews. Jeroboam took the majority of subjects and formed a separate monarchy to the north.

• *Foreign adversaries.* Most of Solomon's reign was free from external threat. But as a consequence of Solomon's sin, God heated up the cold wars with old foes of Israel. Two soldiers who had unsuccessfully clashed with King David—Hadad and Razon—were hot on the trail of revenge. The Bible doesn't describe any skirmishes between Israel and the two marauding bands of outlaws. But we get the idea that their harassment kept Solomon and his advisers from getting a good night's sleep.

• *Despair and heartache.* Perhaps the most sobering outcome of Solomon's self-indulgence was personal boredom and emptiness. Contrary to what you might think, life lost its luster for Solomon. The pleasures of fame, money, and sex didn't have staying power. Solomon's description of their long-range impact on his life belongs on the marquee of every X-rated theater and the bottle of every illegal drug: "I did not withhold my heart from any pleasure . . . I considered all my activities . . . and behold all was vanity and striving after wind and there was no profit under the sun" (Ecc. 2:10-12).

I've talked to young adults who claim that their defiance of God's laws hasn't caused a minute's pain. Maybe they're telling the truth. But I can't help but wonder: what will they write in *their* journals a few years down the road?

Solomon had the "good life" by the tail—and it bit him! I came across the following story in a text analyzing the Old Testament Book of Ecclesiastes (the title of Solomon's journal). Note its irony:

E. Stanley Jones, in his book *Growing Spiritually*, talks about a fictional person who lived out a fantasy life. All he had to do was think of it and (poof!) it happened. So this man, in a moment of time, sticks his hands in his pockets and leans back and imagines a mansion and (poof!) he has a fifteen-bedroom mansion, three stories with servants instantly available to wait upon his every need.

Why, a place like that needs several fine cars. So he again closes his eyes and imagines the driveway full of the finest wheels money can buy. And (poof!) there are several of the best vehicles instantly brought before his mind's eye. He is free to drive them himself, or sit way back in the limousine with that mafia glass wrapped around the rear, and have the chauffeur drive him wherever he wishes.

There's no other place to travel so he comes back home and wishes for a sumptuous meal and (poof!) there's the meal in front of him with all of its mouth-watering aromas and beauty—which he eats alone. And yet . . . there was something more he needed to find happiness.

Finally, he grows so terribly bored and unchallenged that he whispers to one of the attendants, "I want to get out of this. I want to create some things again. I'd rather be in *hell* than be here." To which one of the servants replies quietly, "Where do you think you are?"[5]

Let's not kid ourselves. The things that tempted Solomon— and still tempt us—feel good at first. Otherwise, they wouldn't entice us. But the "if-it-feels-good-do it" philosophy of life has a flip slide. It's called hell on earth.

Home Before Dark
I can't close the book on Solomon without one more sobering truth. *How we finish in life is more important than how we start.* Spiritually speaking, Solomon started off on the right foot. But when other things vied for his attention, he faltered before reaching the finish line.

His experience tells us to junk the idea that we've arrived spiritually because of a one-time experience with the Lord, or even because He has greatly used us in the past. Neither a valid conversion experience nor a fruitful ministry insulates us from temptation or the possibility of moral failure. Lots of Christians have scarred their lives because, as they grew older, they became spiritually complacent. They withdrew from faith-strengthening fellowship or stopped tapping into God's power through Bible study and prayer. There's a word for people who take spiritual warfare and holiness for granted: *victim.* The message of Solomon's experience is loud and clear. Let's not cover our ears.

Perhaps my friend, Robertson McQuilkin, had Solomon's plight in mind when he penned the following poem. As a former missionary to Japan, and current Chancellor of Columbia Bible College, he has offered decades of productive service to the Lord. Yet he doesn't presume on the future.

LET ME GET HOME BEFORE DARK

It's sundown, Lord.
The shadows of my life stretch back
    into the dimness of the years long spent.
I fear not death, for that grim foe betrays himself at last,
    thrusting me forever into life:
Life with you, unsoiled and free.
But I do fear.
I fear the Dark Spectre may come too soon —

or do I mean too late?
That I should stain your honor, shame your name,
   grieve your loving heart.
Few, they tell me, finish well . . .
Lord, let me get home before dark.

The darkness of a spirit
   grown mean and small, fruit shriveled on the vine,
   bitter to the taste of my companions,
   burden to be borne by those brave few who love me still.
No, Lord. Let the fruit grow lush and sweet,
   A joy to all who taste;
Spirit-sign of God at work,
   stronger, fuller, brighter at the end.
Lord, let me get home before dark.

The darkness of tattered gifts;
   rust-locked, half-spent or ill-spent,
A life that was once used of God
   now set aside.
Grief for glories gone or
Fretting for a task God never gave.
Mourning in the hollow chambers of memory;
Gazing on the faded banners of victories long gone.
Cannot I run well unto the end?
Lord, let me get home before dark.

The outer me decays —
   I do not fret or ask reprieve.
The ebbing strength but weans me from mother earth
   and grows me up for heaven.
I do not cling closely to shadows cast by immortality.
I do not patch the scaffold lent to build the real, eternal me.
I do not clutch about me my cocoon,
   vainly struggling to hold hostage
   a free spirit pressing to be born.

But will I reach the gate
in lingering pain, body distorted, grotesque?
Or will it be a mind
wandering untethered among light phantasies or grim
terrors?
Of your grace, Father, I humbly ask . . .
Let me get home before dark.

CHAPTER THREE

Open Mouth, Insert Foot

Have you ever found your words difficult to digest? If so, Harvey Driggers can identify with you. He's a radio announcer at WSCQ in Columbia, South Carolina. Several years ago, he and Gene McKay were chatting flippantly over the air about hypothetical situations. Out of the blue, McKay popped this question, "Would you eat a bowl of live crickets for $40,000?"

"Well, yes," Driggers answered.

"For $4,000?" McKay prompted.

"Yes," insisted Driggers.

"How about $150?" McKay inquired.

"No," Driggers replied.

Finally, Driggers conceded that he'd eat a bowl of crickets for as low as $250. The two friends were chuckling about the "Harvey Driggers Cricket Eating Fund" when phones began ringing off the hook. Unsolicited pledges of money for the fund flooded in. Listeners put their money where his mouth was! Local officials even provided a widely-publicized public forum for the cricket-eating event. Days later, hundreds of onlookers gawked as Driggers poured chocolate over a bowl of live crickets and gobbled them down.[1]

Driggers would be the first to vouch for the moral of this story: when we're forced to eat our words, they can be hard to stomach!

Driggers' crunchy snack offers us an innocent chuckle. But as easily as words can spawn the healing effect of laughter, they can just as easily break the human heart. For every harmless boast that spews from our lips, we launch scores of verbal missiles that wreak havoc on relationships. Who hasn't bled after getting in the way of a slashing tongue? Perhaps you still have scars from the last time somebody fired verbal salvos at you.

In his book, *Conversation, Please,* Loren Carroll says, "Most of us devote more time to talking than to any other activity."[2] According to one estimate, we babble between 25,000 and 30,000 words every day. Multiply that figure by the billions of people in the world, and . . . *I don't even want to think about it!*

Over 100 references to the tongue dot the book of Proverbs. Those verses mention the positive as well as the damaging effects of words. Graze on Proverbs 18:21: *"Death* and *life* are in the power of the tongue" (emphasis mine). In this chapter, I'll fixate on sins of the tongue. The next chapter balances the scale by examining the plus side of speech.

What speech defects does Proverbs condemn? What are the most obvious symptoms of foot-in-mouth disease? What destructive consequences do we often leave in the wake of careless words? How can we put a leash on our runaway mouths and minimize the damage?

The following pages beam the spotlight on these questions. One thing's for sure: you'll discover that big-mouthism is *not* a congenital birth defect that a person is saddled with for life. Fasten your seatbelts, and journey with me through Proverbs.

The Truth about Lying

Right up front, God says that He loathes lies. Creating a false impression with words is one of the six things the Lord expressly hates (Prov. 6:16-17). To mislead someone on purpose is "an abomination to the Lord" (Prov. 12:22). Lying lips have a boomerang effect on us because "a false witness will not go unpunished, and he who tells lies will not escape." Without pulling punches, God orders us to "put away from you a deceitful mouth" (Prov. 4:24).

What matters to God is the motive which propels our words. Lying is not only relaying something we know is untrue; it's also choosing words that cause the hearer to believe something that isn't so. What matters to God is not our choice of words, but the intent which spawned those words. It all boils down to this question: is the impression we hope to leave with words an accurate one?

Why do we stretch the truth? To make ourselves look more acceptable to others, or to receive benefits we couldn't claim otherwise? Yet a person who knows Jesus Christ can't lie and enjoy the apparent benefits. To deceive grieves the Holy Spirit, who calls the heart of believers home. Part of the punishment for lying that's promised in Proverbs comes in the form of a joy-sapping twinge of guilt. As one psychologist put it, "Most people feel guilty because they are!"

Believe me, I learned the hard way that lying doesn't pay. The following incident occurred when I was a part-time youth director at a church. Though it took place when I was in grad school—back before the earth's crust hardened—it illustrates the inner turbulence that deceit causes:

"Did you ask your friend if he could sing for us at the banquet?" Jack asked me just before the worship service began.

"Uh—I talked to him Friday," I answered, fidgeting. "He's behind in his studies because he returned late from vacation. He said he'd better not make any more commitments right now."

Jack nodded. "Thanks a lot for asking him," he said, returning to his seat. I stared blankly at the bulletin in my hand, bewildered. I had lied. I *had* talked to my friend the week before, but I had forgotten to ask him about singing at the banquet. Something inside would not let me admit my failure to Jack.

There I was: the church youth director, devoted to full-time Christian service, squirming in my seat, too upset to even sing a hymn. A few years ago I probably wouldn't have given it another thought. But now my life had been surrendered to God. His Holy Spirit was convicting me. By the time the sermon began, the weight of the guilt was more than I could bear. I left my seat, tiptoed to where Jack sat, and motioned him outside. There I admitted my lie and asked his forgiveness.[3]

Confessing to Jack wasn't easy. But to my surprise, his respect for me mushroomed rather than diminished. Though I felt lower than a snake's belly in a wagon rut, at least I had modeled how to handle a lie.

Slanderous Speech

How does God feel about a slanderer? Set your scope on Proverbs 10:18: "He who spreads slander is a fool." Maybe He's blunt because of the disastrous effect slander has on relationships: "A slanderer separates intimate friends" (16:28).

Crack open a dictionary, and you get the idea that *slander* refers only to *false* oral statements which ruin a person's reputation. It appears to be a specific form of lying that mars a third party's image. But *Webster's Dictionary* isn't our inspired source, Proverbs is. And the biblical word we translate as *slander* has a different shade of meaning. The Hebrew word includes *true* as well as false remarks. No one explains the term better than Carole Mayhall:

> In the Old Testament the word *slander* was used for bad reports in general. The Hebrew word meaning "to defame or strip one of his positive reputation" was used in the account of Joseph's true but "bad report" to his father concerning the wickedness of his brothers (Genesis 37:2).

The same word was used in Numbers 13:32, the account of the ten spies who brought back a negative report about the Promised Land.

In the New Testament, the word for slander is comprised of two words, one meaning "against" and the other meaning "to speak." A slanderer, then, is simply one who speaks against another. Slander is the *open, intentional sharing of damaging information* and is characterized by bad reports that blemish or defame a person's reputation *whether they are true or not!*[4]

Here's the bottom line: just because it's true doesn't mean we should announce it over a public address system. Before we add juicy tidbits to a conversation about somebody, let's apply the guidelines in Ephesians 4:29: "Let no unwholesome word proceed from your mouth, but only such a word as is good for edification according to the need of the moment, that it may give grace to those who hear." Unless we heed those conversational criteria, our gossipy chat becomes nothing more than "acid indiscretion."

I heard about a Christian couple in Texas who often entertained guests. They became concerned about the tendency of so many conversations to erode. The talk would often shift to criticisms of people who weren't present. They tried to resolve the problem by hanging a huge plaque above the mantle of the fireplace. It reads: THE ABSENT ONE IS SAFE AMONG US.

Rash Remarks

Another symptom of a foot-shaped mouth detected by the probing X-rays of Proverbs is hasty or impulsive speech—exercising the lips without activating the brain. Proverbs 12:18 compares rash speech to "the thrusts of a sword." Solomon also denounced the tendency to give a verbal reply before hearing all the facts: "He who gives an answer before he hears, it is folly and shame to him" (Prov. 18:13). Careless words also clip your future's wings. Nobody with loose lips makes it to the top of his profession. "Do you see a man who is hasty in his words? There is more hope for a fool than for him" (Prov. 29:20).

Harvey Driggers, the cricket-munching disc jockey, isn't the only radio announcer who has muttered hasty words over the air. When the Pittsburgh Pirates baseball team took a 10-0 first-inning lead over the Philadelphia Phillies back in June 1989, broadcaster Jim Rooker said, "If the Pirates lose this game, I'll walk back to Pittsburgh."

The lead seemed insurmountable, so Rooker figured his comment about the 288-mile cross-state hike was safe. But the Phillies must have gotten word of Rooker's boast. They rallied for a 15-11 win. As soon as the season ended, Rooker arranged for pledges to benefit Children's Hospital, then wore out a pair of walking shoes between the two Pennsylvania cities. He may be the first person ever whose primary symptom of foot-in-mouth disease was aching feet.[5]

Tone It Down!

You're aware that *how* we say something often packs more of a wallop than *what* we say. Perhaps more than any other tongue problem, a harsh tone of voice rips and tears like shrapnel in the hearer's heart. When we turn the volume of our voice up too high, others merely plug their ears and go on the defensive: "A gentle answers turns away wrath, but a harsh word stirs up anger" (Prov. 15:1).

Experts tell us that of all the thoughts and feelings we communicate in a conversation:

- 7 percent is communicated by the actual words we say;
- 38 percent is transmitted by *how* we deliver those words (tone of voice);
- 55 percent is conveyed by nonverbal cues (gestures, facial expressions, etc.).

Imagine—our tone of voice carries five time more comfort or hurt than our actual words!

A disturbing tone of voice usually stems from the soil of anger. Proverbs acknowledges the inevitable conflicts among people. That's why Solomon advises us to put a muzzle over our mouths whenever we're upset: "Abandon the quarrel before it breaks out" (Prov. 17:14). "Keeping away from strife is an honor for a man, but any fool will quarrel" (Prov. 20:3).

I vividly recall a knock-down, drag-out fist fight between my brother and me when I was 19. I don't remember what we argued about, but the razor-sharp words I shouted at him will echo forever in my memory: "Dennis, I *hate* you!"

In the 20 years since that quarrel, Dennis and I haven't seen much of each other. Do my harsh words still sting him like they do me? If *only* I could take them back. . . .

I discovered the truth of a quip by Henry Ward Beecher, a 19th century preacher: "Speak when you are angry and you'll make the best speech you'll ever regret."

Verbal Overflow
The final tongue problem we'll hoist from the pages of Proverbs is hinted at by a drab gray tombstone in an old English church-yard. When you stoop over and look closely, the faint etchings reveal this epitaph:

BENEATH THIS STONE, A LUMP OF CLAY,
LIES ARABELLA YOUNG,
WHO, ON THE TWENTY – FOURTH OF MAY,
BEGAN TO HOLD HER TONGUE.[6]

What does Proverbs say about talking too much? "When there are many words, transgression is unavoidable, but he who restrains his lips is wise" (10:19). What are the consequences of wordiness? "The one who guards his mouth preserves his life; the one who opens wide his lips comes to ruin" (13:3).

To put it another way, we "save face" by keeping the lower half shut! Former senator Ed Muskie echoed the sentiment of Proverbs when he said, "Do not speak unless you can improve the silence." I'm not suggesting you turn into a wallflower. The point is *control*, not a squirt of Super Glue between your lips.

The matter of control reminds me of James 3:8: "No one can tame the tongue." Whoa . . . did he mean that it's useless to try to change our conversational habits? Is a diseased mouth terminal? No. If taming the tongue were impossible, God wouldn't hold us responsible for our words. Yet He does. Jesus Himself said, "Every careless word that men shall speak, they shall render account for it in the day of judgment" (Matt. 12:36). James' point is this: we can't lick tongue problems on our own apart from supernatural reinforcements.

Then how do we call on those reinforcements? If you're serious about winning the war against wayward words, heed the following battle strategies.

Oral Hygiene

1. *If the light of Proverbs has exposed any form of sinful speech, confess it to God.* To confess something simply means to agree with God's assessment of it. Overcoming a destructive verbal habit begins by admitting it's wrong. Whenever the Holy Spirit pricks our conscience over a remark, we can choose one of two responses: stubbornly carry the burden of guilt ourselves, or confess it to Jesus and forget about it. "If we confess our sins, He is faithful and righteous to forgive us our sins and to cleanse us from all unrighteousness" (1 John 1:9).

2. *Yield control of your tongue to God on a daily basis.* A single prayer of confession gets you off on the right foot. Yet watching what we say must become a lifestyle. Shooting one prayer to heaven won't immunize us to the germs in a diseased tongue. David recognized that we must take the antidote in regular doses for the rest of our lives. His words in Psalm 39:1 acknowledge the continuing process that's involved: "I will guard my ways, that I may not sin with my tongue; I will guard my mouth as with a muzzle."

3. *Give the Holy Spirit something to work with by memorizing Scripture.* If our lips are sore from too much exercise, we can store in our hearts two verses previously quoted in this chapter: Proverbs 10:19 and Ephesians 4:29. Put the verses on notecards

where you'll see them everyday—by the phone, on a bulletin board, or inside a notebook.

4. *Seek a prescription for the root problem, not just for the symptoms.* Wayward words are symptoms of a deeper malady. They reveal an infected heart. Warren Wiersbe tells about a professing Christian "who got angry on the job and let loose with some oaths. Embarrassed, he turned to his partner and said, 'I don't know why I said that. It really isn't in me.' But his partner wisely replied, 'It had to be in you or it couldn't have come out of you.' "[7] Jesus stressed the same point: "The good man out of the good treasure of his heart brings forth what is good; and the evil man out of the evil treasure brings forth what is evil; *for his mouth speaks from that which fills his heart*" (Luke 6:45, emphasis mine).

How do you determine if an infection plagues your body? Pop a thermometer in your mouth. If the mercury zooms to 100-plus, you know you're being invaded by hostile germs. Body temperature is a so-called "vital sign of health." How can you tell if you're sick spiritually? Look at your conversational patterns through the lens of Scripture. For the tongue is "the thermometer of the heart."

This closing perspective suggests that putting a reign on verbal vices, as well as harnessing the tongue's positive potential, is impossible without a growing relationship with Jesus Christ. Sometimes we launch quickie prayers up to Jesus, asking for self-control and patience in our speech without exhibiting a gut-level desire to know Him better. Yet Christlike qualities don't come packaged separately. They're a by-product of a love relationship with Him. Ways we cultivate that relationship include regular times of prayer, Bible study, and rubbing elbows with other Christians.

Remember—if it is to be healed, a feverish mouth requires good rapport with a heart specialist.

CHAPTER FOUR
Conversation Under Construction

When it comes to making garbled or muddled comments, sports personalities come in first place. A former Hall of Fame catcher and baseball manager, Yogi Berra is still the king of confusing observations. "Ninety percent of baseball is half mental," he once asserted. A teammate, Bobby Richardson, wondered why Yogi carried so much life insurance. "Gee, Bobby, you don't know nothing about money," snapped Berra. "I'll get it all back when I die."

While they were enjoying lunch in a New York restaurant, Berra once said to Richardson, "Don't look now, but somebody famous is sitting behind you."

"Who is it?" Richardson inquired.

"I'm not sure," Yogi answered. "I get them confused. There are two of them, brothers. One died. I'm not sure which one that is behind you, the one that died or the other one."

Curt Young had his moments, too. The former Oakland A's pitcher, after serving up a Herculean home run to Reggie Jackson, observed, "He really jumped on it. He hit it a lot farther than it went."

And here's how Bo Belinsky, another major league hurler,

explained a string of successful performances: "Right now I feel that I've got my feet on the ground as far as my head is concerned."

Baseball players don't own the franchise on fuzzy remarks, though. Any lineup of verbal All-Stars includes Bill Peterson, former Florida State and Houston Oilers football coach. In a terse reply to fans who second-guessed him, he said, "I'm the football coach around here, and don't you remember it!" He had his more solemn moments, too. Before an important game, Peterson asked the FSU captain to "please lead us in a few words of silent prayer."[1]

Despite those offbeat comments from the lips of athletes, the tongue is a marvel of creation. Though it's the world's smallest but most powerful troublemaker, as illustrated in the last chapter, the tongue also offers welcome words. Proverbs portrays its positive potential, too.

You can improve upon the verbal execution of Yogi Berra and company. Apply this chapter on the healing power of speech, and you'll earn post-season honors in the conversation department. The pages that follow tell how to tame your talk and win with words.

The Encouragement Connection
Rivet your attention on the following excerpts from Proverbs. In your own words, to what positive purpose of speech do they refer?

Anxiety in the heart of a man weighs it down, but a good word makes it glad (12:25).

A soothing tongue is a tree of life (15:4).

Pleasant words are a honeycomb, sweet to the soul and healing to the bones (16:24).

Those verses zero in on the capacity of words to encourage or lift the spirits of others. New Testament references piggyback on this point from Proverbs. As far as the Apostle Paul was concerned, vocal encouragement is a command, not an option among Christians: "'Encourage one another, and build up one another" (1 Thess. 5:11).

Author Virgil Vogt employs a modern-day analogy to illustrate this ministry of the mouth.

The New Testament Greek word for encouragement contains the idea of being called alongside another. On the coldest winter days we do this to some of our cars. When one battery is so weak that it cannot spark its engine, we bring another car alongside and connect the working battery with heavy jumper cables to the weaker battery. Nothing is changed in the car that won't start. But with the direct infusion of power from the other vehicle, the weakness is overcome and the stranded car is able to function on its own.

We Christians often need to connect with the strength in others in order to get started or to keep going in difficult circumstances. We need someone to come alongside and give us a "jump."[2]

When the energy oozes out of the batteries of folks around you, how can you infuse them with power to keep going? You give others a "jump" when you:

- compliment a character trait or course of action you've observed in them
- tell them how something they said or did spurred you on spiritually
- say taken-for-granted things such as "I'm your friend," "I'm willing to listen," or "I care about you."
- defend them against unfair criticism
- call to find out why they missed Sunday School or your fellowship outing
- pray with them over a need they've expressed

● share an answer to prayer, or a helpful insight God has shown you from the Bible

● describe the vacancy they'd leave in your life if they were no longer around

Paying Off Debts of Gratitude

A first cousin to encouragement is expressing appreciation. When someone else meets a need or fills a vacuum in your life, do you thank him or her for the contribution to your joy? The last chapter of Proverbs lists the chores and characteristics of a godly wife and mother. With a final dip of his pen into the inkwell, the writer describes the reaction of her family members: "Her children rise up and bless her; her husband also, and he praises her, saying: 'Many daughters have done nobly, but you excel them all' " (Prov. 31:28-29).

They didn't just *feel* grateful—they voiced their appreciation. Dad and the kids unlocked the private vault where feelings were stored and enriched Mom's life through praise. We can't tiptoe around their example. Let's convert warm fuzzy thoughts about people into words. Our legitimate praise may catapult them even closer to their potential as persons.

Back in college, while waiting for a date in the dorm lobby one evening, I flipped through an old magazine. I forget the name of the periodical, but the cartoon caption I spotted is as clear today as it was twenty years ago. Etched on a tombstone were these words:

HERE LIES A MAN WHO WAS ALWAYS
"GOING TO . . . "
NOW HE'S GONE.

Every time I'm tempted to put off a word of gratitude or appreciation, that caption surfaces in my mind. It reminds me that opportunities to exercise this ministry of the tongue are limited. Before I know it, a long distance move—or even death—could bury the chance to say what's on my heart. Is there anyone to whom you owe gratitude, or to whom you've intended to pay a compliment? Does the face of a relative or close friend flash on the screen of your mind? I'm not trying to be morbid, but here's a maxim worth remembering: *no one can smell the flowers on his coffin!*

Pass It On
He spoke the words almost two decades ago, in an address to the student body at Wheaton College. Every time I glean a new insight from a book, a Sunday School class, or devotions, his words goad me into action. They keep me from becoming selfish about what I learn.

God never teaches you solely for your own benefit.

Pastor Stuart Briscoe was saying that we're supposed to pass along the spiritual truths we come across. Solomon would agree. Proverbs makes it clear that God designed tongues as tools for teaching: "The lips of the righteous feed many, but fools die for lack of understanding" (10:21). He reinforced the point later on: "The lips of the wise spread knowledge, but the hearts of fools are not so" (15:7). Before leaving the subject, Solomon described the priceless nature of talk that teaches: "There is gold, and an abundance of jewels; but the lips of knowledge are a more precious thing" (20:15).

Does this mean God expects you to get a seminary degree and stand behind a lectern the rest of your life? No. Proverbs isn't referring to teaching in just a public, formal sense. And you don't need an ordination certificate on the wall before you can share truth from God's Word. Your tongue teaches whenever you:

● tell a friend or relative how to become a Christian.

● recount to members of your Bible study group an example of God's faithfulness to you.

● recite within earshot of others what the speaker said during the last retreat.

● explain a Bible lesson to kids during children's church or Vacation Bible School.

● share an encouraging truth uncovered during your personal Bible reading.

● read someone a book excerpt that pricked your conscience, or put a match to your spiritual fervor.

● explain how a truth or verse from the Bible helped you make a decision.

That's the non-professional kind of teaching Paul had in mind when he wrote, "Let the word of Christ richly dwell within you, with all wisdom teaching and admonishing one another" (Col. 3:16). There's only one qualification: regular exposure to God's truth. If you're learning, you have something to say.

Recently, I spotted an eye-popping photo in a newspaper that reminded me to balance the input I'm getting with output. The Associated Press photo depicted a muscular 32-year-old Britisher pulling a Concorde jet at London's Heathrow Airport. The strong man is David Gauder. He pulled the Concorde a total of 40 feet from a stationary position. According to the caption, Gauder has also pulled a 40-ton tractor-trailer, halted powerboats, and prevented two small aircraft from taking off—one strapped to each arm!

The article accompanying the photo divulged the eating habits of the 5'7" 240-pound Achilles. Gauder's *daily diet* consists of 25 eggs, five pounds of bananas, a whole chicken, six pints of milk, baked potatoes, and two 32-ounce steaks. Just digesting that much food takes lots of effort![3]

Despite his caloric intake, Gauder is a model physical specimen. Yet imagine what he'd look like if he swallowed all that food without working out regularly. In no time, flab would replace his rock-hard muscle.

Similarly, when we taste a steady diet of Bible truth, yet keep it to ourselves, we eventually become spiritually weak and flabby. The only way to burn off the calories and keep our spiritual figure trim is to exercise the lips. Sharing God's life-sustaining food with others is like converting calories into energy. In the spiritual as well as the physical realm, the principle is inescapable: *health requires a balance between input and output.*

More Verbal Lessons

The plus side of speech in Proverbs includes at least two additional verbal lessons. Proverbs 22:11 salutes the individual "whose speech is *gracious*." To speak graciously means to offer verbal gifts even when the recipients don't deserve them. It's treating the person to whom or about whom we're talking better than they've treated us. Another verbal exercise Solomon recommends is a *well-timed word*: "A man has joy in an apt answer, and how delightful is a timely word" (15:23). "Like apples of gold in settings of silver is a word spoken in right circumstances" (25:11). Obeying those verses requires sensitivity to the needs of folks around us and an awareness of their teachable moments. It means allowing their nonverbal cues to tell us when to turn the ignition to the motors in our mouths.

My senior year in high school, my English teacher timed her words perfectly. I didn't think much of myself at the time. I considered myself the type of person who could brighten up any room—by *leaving it*, if you know what I mean! Report cards publicized my aversion to study, and I had no intention of going to college.

Enter Mrs. Spratt. She found a poem I had written and left lying on my desk. What a shock when she began class the next day by reading it out loud! In front of twenty classmates, she turned to me and predicted: "I can see it now. In a few years, you'll earn a degree in journalism. And someday the rest of us will read the poems and books you write. I'm not going to let you waste this God-given ability!"

Her kind words spawned an 180-degree turnaround. After that incident, I put more effort into school—especially my English assignments. I cracked the books more often to please the first person who ever believed in me. Eventually, her prophecies about a journalism degree and a writing career were fulfilled.

Is That a Trowel in Your Mouth?

A trowel is a tool with a handle and a flat, sharp-pointed blade. Bricklayers use it to spread mortar between bricks. Whoever invented the trowel obviously designed it for a *constructive* purpose, but you could use it to damage property or to hurt somebody.

When I wonder why God gave us tongues, I remember the trowel. Both the trowel and the tongue can slash a person to pieces. Yet both were created for the purpose of building up, rather than for tearing down.

There's a trowel in your mouth. How are you using it?

CHAPTER FIVE

How to Make
Wise Choices

I've watched folks make some foolish choices in my time. And I've made my share of boners. Yet the judgments handed down in the following court cases deserve top ranking in the "Absurd Decisions" category. I don't know if the presiding judges and juries had cobwebs in their craniums, but something obstructed the normal flow of brain juice.

● In New York City, a man tried to commit suicide by jumping in the path of a subway train. Though badly injured, he survived. Then he sued the subway authority and collected $650,000 in damages!

● When a man tried to rob a school, he fell through a skylight. He sued the school district over the injuries. The district's insurance company had to dish out $260,000, plus $1,500 per month indefinitely. For him, crime paid handsomely.

● A drunk driver caromed off a curb and plowed into a telephone booth. The person using the phone sustained injuries. Who did California's chief justice hold responsible for the accident? The company that designed the telephone booth!

● Two men needed a trimmer for the hedge that separated their lots. One of them bought a lawn mower from Sears. The

49

neighbors lifted the lawn mower, and actually tried using it, instead of a hedge trimmer, to cut the shrubbery. The heavy mower slipped from their grasp, and the blade slashed two fingers from one man's hand. Were they embarrassed for using a push mower in such a foolish fashion? Nope. The injured man sued Sears for *not* telling him that the machine was *not* a hedge cutter. He won a large monetary settlement.[1]

Sounds like somebody trimmed the common sense off the minds of those decision-makers. A little wisdom would've gone a long way to insure justice.

Even if you're never tabbed for jury duty or never don a judge's robe, you still need to know how to make sensible choices. Your decision-making ability may already be on trial. Should you take the promotion, though it requires moving the family and severing the kids' ties with their friends? Is the career change that's been percolating in your brain your last chance for vocational fulfillment, or a whim fueled by a mid-life crisis? What sort of consequences should you impose for the varying degrees of rebellion or irresponsibility exhibited by your kids? How will you come up with the cash needed for their college education? Should you put your ailing mother in a nursing home or accept the rigors of caring for her in your own house?

When the time comes to make such decisions, hopefully you'll exercise better judgment than the courts did in the previously cited lawsuits. One way to increase the likelihood of making sound judgments is to digest what Proverbs says about the decision-making process. Proverbs contains scores of verses focusing on topics such as the future, handling uncertainty, planning, and making choices. From those references we can glean principles of decision-making that are as up-to-date as political upheavals in Eastern Europe and recruiting scandals in college athletics. Mastering this chapter won't make planning and choosing a breeze. But it will provide shock absorbers to make your ride into the future a bit smoother.

After all, you should be concerned about the future. That's where you'll be spending the rest of your life.

Gift-wrapping Your Future

The insight required for smart decisions isn't dispensed across a drugstore counter. Whether or not we exercise sound judgment depends a lot on whom we consult for help. Do we rely on our own wits, or do we plug into divine discernment?

Decision-making principle #1 is the most basic thing Proverbs says on the subject: *The most reliable source of wisdom for making sensible choices is God.* I'm not saying that an unbeliever who never cracks a Bible or mutters a prayer can't make a right decision now and then. Within every human being God created some degree of common sense. Yet when push comes to shove, the know-how needed for a consistent pattern of sane choices stems from an ongoing relationship with our Creator. The closer we are to Him, the more we're apt to think and to react like Him—to view alternatives through the 20-20 lens of His Word.

Employing God as our primary consultant requires us to gift-wrap our future, and offer it to Him—no strings attached. Those who give God their future discover that they get back a more purposeful and adventuresome version of that future. Other perspectives on decision-making from Proverbs won't make sense unless God has ownership of our lives.

"Commit your works to the Lord," Solomon advised, "and your plans will be established" (Prov. 16:3). Have *you* made a rational commitment of your future to the Lord? Have you given Him an OK to design the blueprint for your tomorrow? We can't waltz around this truth: *tapping into His wisdom requires transferring the deed to our life over to God.* Only then will we view each separate decision on the basis of how it fits into the big picture of His will. Only then will we make regular appointments with Him as a means of discovering His perspective on things. Whether you're thirty years old or sixty, *it's never too late to do what is right!* "Those who seek the Lord understand all things," insisted Solomon (Prov. 28:5).

Look at it this way. Wisdom is a by-product of personal integrity. When tough choices confront us, we can trust our intuition a lot more if we're living close to God. "The integrity of the upright will guide them" (Prov. 11:3).

As spiritual as all this sounds, trusting your future to the Lord isn't something that comes naturally. To relinquish control of the future to God is gut-wrenching for some folks. Here's an honest inquiry of a young adult:

Trust you with my life?

God, that's the same as saying,
"Here, it's yours now."
And I'm not sure I'm ready for that.

I'm afraid to say, "You take over, God."
It's risky.
What will happen to *my* plans?
I have my own ideas about
which job offer to take
where to live
how to spend my money and leisure time
what to do during retirement.
I want to be sure
before I yield my future to You
that You won't spoil things for me.

God, if I trust You with my life,
What would You do with it?[2]

If you can identify with this poem, mull over God's reply to the poet's question: "Trust in the Lord with all your heart, and do not lean on your own understanding. In all your ways acknowledge Him, and *He will make your paths straight*" (Prov. 3:5-6, emphasis mine).

The Future in Present Tense

Centuries ago a small band of Roman invaders landed on the shores of what is now England. Defenders of the island had successfully repelled attempts by other groups to wrest away control of the area. When the defenders first spotted the new invaders, they strutted around confidently, figuring they had their number. Then the natives witnessed an eye-popping spectacle that changed their cocky attitude. What they saw melted their hearts and siphoned off their confidence. Before moving inland, the Roman soldiers burned every one of their own boats! Retreat was no longer an alternative. It was forward or die!

The Roman soldiers were "thinking in the future tense." Their plans to take over the island dominated their present behavior. With that objective in mind, they pondered this question: "What can we do *now* in order to increase the likelihood of success?" That's when they burned the boats. They knew they'd fight harder if escape wasn't an option.

Their mode of decision-making illustrates planning principle #2: *Think through the effect future goals and needs should have on current choices.* I call this the art of "putting the future into the present tense." Our tendency is to bracket off the present from the future. We usually make choices based on current benefits rather than long-term consequences. But Proverbs makes it clear that reaching tomorrow's goals should affect the way we operate now. (After all, it wasn't raining when Noah began construction on the ark. But he knew he'd be in over his head if he waited until the first raindrop fell!)

Proverbs uses the ant, a hard-working son, and a housewife to show that effective decision-making requires "thinking in the future tense." First, the author compliments the ant for anticipating future needs, then working in the present to meet those needs: "Go to the ant, O sluggard, observe her ways and be wise, which, having no chief, officer or ruler, prepares her food in the summer, and gathers her provision in the harvest" (Prov. 6:6-8). He employed the same agricultural analogy to salute the diligence of a young man: "He who gathers in summer is a son who acts wisely, but he who sleeps in harvest is a son who acts shamefully" (10:5). Food on the table in January was dependent on a certain course of behavior in August.

The housewife portrayed in Proverbs 31 also made choices in the present based on her anticipation of the future. She could smile at the prospect of winter blizzards, because during short-sleeve weather she made scarlet overcoats for family members (31:19-22).

You may think that the illustrations in Proverbs are as out of date as hula-hoops and Mercury dimes. You don't sweat a lot over what you'll eat or wear six months down the road. But the point is timeless: *get in the habit of mulling over current implications of future needs and aspirations.* If you heed this principle, you'll be the exception rather than the rule. Most of us play fast and loose with our future. We tend to think that time moves with the speed of a glacier, when in reality it darts by with the quickness of Carl Lewis during a 100-yard dash. Before you know it, we're eyeball to eyeball with the future for which we have failed to prepare.

Let's get specific. If you're a parent and your child's college education is looming on the horizon, the following information is an eye-opener. According to a national survey of teens in the United States, choosing a college and a career are their biggest concerns. Yet saving money for college isn't in vogue: 77 percent of 742 teens surveyed say they've saved no money toward their future education. Half of the respondents also said their folks didn't have the money. Their lack of savings, though, isn't due to a lack of resources. Most of the teens who responded work part-time, earning $50-$100 per week. They reported spending their money on clothes, stereos, movie tickets, and car expenses.[3]

Teens' spending habits aren't necessarily a matter of right and wrong. Don't think Proverbs is advocating a miserly existence for them now as a way to bankroll the future. Yet don't miss the point: these teens reported worrying about funds for college, yet few put aside even a small portion of their earnings to increase their likelihood of enrolling. That's enslavement to the present. They're aware of future needs, yet fail to make current choices in light of those needs. That kind of reasoning is as solid as quicksand. Besides, should *we* parents sacrifice financially if our employed teens aren't willing to pitch in? How can we share this decision-making insight with them? Is requiring them to save a portion of their earnings a valid application?

Don't think teens are the only target group who need this second principle, though. What needs do you spot when you look at *your* future? What goals do you have for the next five to ten years? What effect should these needs and goals have on your current behavior and choices? Don't let *your* future become a time when you wish you'd have done what you aren't doing now. When you're dying of thirst, it's too late to think about digging a well.

Painful Presumption
Perhaps the greatest magician and escape artist of all time was Harry Houdini. His feats would have made even David Copperfield stand up and clap. Within seconds he could break out of any handcuff, straightjacket, or jail cell.

Except one. Officials of a jail in the British Isles finally out-smarted him. Houdini toyed with the cell door lock for over two hours. He had picked similar locks in as little as three seconds. But nothing he tried worked. Finally, he gave up and slumped exhaustedly against the cell door. It swung open. The door to the jail cell had never been locked![4]

The normally shrewd escape artist *presumed* the cell door was locked, without investigating the matter. He took for granted that they wouldn't ask him to escape from a jail cell that was unlocked. He supposed a basic fact to be true without checking for proof.

Houdini's presumption reminds me of decision-making princi-ple #3: *Avoid hasty choices based primarily on presumption or subjective feelings. Get all the facts you can to aid in the decision-making process.* Just ask Houdini: taking the facts for granted only leads to embarrassment.

According to Proverbs 13:10, "Through presumption comes nothing but strife." Presumption is proceeding on the basis of whim or emotion, apart from rational thought about the alternatives. It's figuring something is true, or will work out OK, without evidence or proof. Sometimes a gut feeling steers us in the right direction. Yet Proverbs warns against trying to escape into the future without first checking to see if the door is locked. In contrast to the person who presumes on the future, "every prudent man acts with knowledge" (Prov. 13:16), and a wise planner "acquires knowledge" (18:15). That's another way of saying that he gets all the information he can and proceeds cautiously when choosing among alternatives. He doesn't beat around the bush when it's time to choose. Yet neither does he take a rash step without checking out the ground and where his foot will land.

To transport this planning concept from the domain of theory to the realm of practice, let's look at some examples of presumptuous choices. Instead of researching the facts or acting prudently, the following folks took too much for granted:

• Soon after their wedding, Bob and Fran went into deep debt for a house. They planned to wait several years before having children. They figured her secretarial salary would help make the house payment until Bob's new travel agency got off the ground and provided enough income for Fran to stay home. But six months later, an unplanned pregnancy accompanied by physical complications forced Fran to quit her job. The only way they could stay afloat financially was to sell their dream house and move into a small apartment. The odds of succeeding with their birth control method were almost a hundred to one. But since it wasn't a sure thing, taking on a house payment based on two incomes was a presumptious move.

• When it came to mental fidelity in marriage, Fred, a Christian, was determined to exercise high moral standards. On an out-of-town business trip, he went to see an R-rated movie at the local cinema. The new movie featured his favorite actor, and promised lots of hair-raising adventure. Fred figured that the new release was tagged "R" solely because of violence. Fred knew he was vulnerable to lust when exposed to sex scenes, but the actor involved wasn't known as a sex symbol. Nor had the actor's previous movies included sexually-explicit content. Yet in this movie, sandwiched between the hero's daring efforts to capture drug lords, was a steamy bedroom scene that amounted to soft-core pornography. Ever since that evening, Fred says he has struggled more with his thought life because of flashbacks to that two-minute clip. He informed a friend that he wouldn't have gone if he'd known the movie was so offensive to his values. But finding out in advance about the sexual content of the film was as simple as asking a few questions or reading a review. He didn't acquire the information that was readily available.

• As a college freshman, Pete earned $400 a month on a part-time job. Since first-year courses posed no problems for him, he worked twenty hours a week. Before enrolling for his sophomore year, he went into debt for a new car. He concluded that he made enough to cover the monthly payment and insurance. What he didn't figure on, though, was a tougher slate of courses his second year. The extra academic burden forced him to cut back on his employment and put him in a financial squeeze. He sold the car at a loss, all because he made a purchase choice rooted in presumption rather than facts. Pete opted for the car based on the previous year's academic load. Before assuming such a large debt, he should have investigated the rigors of the more complex sophomore courses and the reputations of a new set of professors.

These scenarios show that the heavenly advice from Proverbs is as down-to-earth as artificial turf on an athletic field. So before you or your offspring reserve a dorm room at the university, visit the campus and uncover all the pluses and minuses. Take a list of questions for students you run into, as well as for the administrators you meet. Don't assume anything unless you've substantiated it with research. And before you let anyone slip an engagement ring on your finger, make sure you have the lowdown on his character. If you wear his diamond because he looks like a matinee idol, figuring he'll change his bad habits after a trip to the altar, that's presumption. You'll get hitched to a headache instead of a hunk. Neither should you take the new job offer in another state without obtaining relevant information. Will higher housing costs deplete what looks like a substantial salary increase? Do you assume you'll enjoy the same job perks and freedom as before without investigating the facts?

As you can see, avoiding presumption boils down to using common sense. But large numbers of adults who regret presumptuous choices will tell you that good sense isn't as common as we like to think.

Don't Be a Lone Ranger

Recently I faced a dilemma about my thirteen-year-old's lackadaisical attitude toward school. How could I encourage a turnabout in his study habits? Before imposing consequences for declining grades, I consulted with Jack. He's a Christian friend who has raised several teens and who has served as a high school principal. I was leaning toward canceling my boy's membership at a local gym until grades improved. If Stephen studied half as conscientiously as he lifts weights, he'd make the honor roll. But Jack cautioned me to think twice about that alternative.

"How does Stephen benefit from the workouts?" Jack inquired.

"It's his only form of regular exercise," I replied. "And he's on the heavy side. I'm afraid he'd be a couch potato without the weight training. Besides, his strength is important to his self-esteem. It's one area in which he towers above his peers."

"Then don't tamper with something that is so good for him," Jack said. After informing Jack that Stephen watched an hour of TV each evening, he advised me to take away TV privileges until grades go up. "Television doesn't profit him the way exercise does," Jack concluded.

As I look back on it, the right parental move in that situation seems clear-cut. But when I'm smack-dab in the middle of a frustrating circumstance, my thinking often gets muddled. Jack's input illustrates decision-making principle #4: *Avoid a lone-ranger approach to solving dilemmas. As you proceed through the process of deciding or planning, get counsel from others.*

Jesus never intended for any of his followers to go it alone. That's why the New Testament uses terms like *family* and *body* to describe the church. From day one He planned for believers to relate closely to one another and help each other along on the journey to maturity. "We belong to each other, and each needs all the others," Paul insisted (Rom. 12:5, TLB).

Solomon made the same point hundreds of years earlier. Proverbs 17:17 salutes the value of a friend to support us and offer perspective during trials: "A friend loves at all times, and a brother is born for adversity." Staying sharp spiritually requires the kind of feedback a friend or adviser can give: "Iron sharpens iron, so one man sharpens another" (Prov. 27:17).

Whether or not we seek others' guidance has a lot to do with future success: "Where there is no guidance, the people fall, but in abundance of counselors there is victory" (Prov. 11:14). "Without consultation, plans are frustrated, but with many counselors they succeed" (Prov. 15:22). God doesn't josh around. Notice what He calls the person who's too proud to seek advice: "The way of a fool is right in his own eyes, but a wise man is he who listens to counsel" (Prov. 12:15).

Proverbs isn't telling you to mooch off others' ideas to the point of becoming indecisive yourself. Whether to go back to work when the kids get older or which college savings plan you should adopt are decisions that ultimately fall in *your* lap. The Book of Proverbs merely encourages you to rely on sources outside yourself to increase the likelihood of choosing wisely.

If you give your future to God and ask Him for wisdom as needed (principle #1), consider the impact future goals and needs should have on current operating procedure (principle #2), find out the facts so you'll know what you're getting into (principle #3), and obtain objective feedback from people you trust (principle #4), then the odds are in your favor.

Of course, the caliber of counsel you receive depends on the quality of the person you consult. Trying to squeeze wisdom from a hollow mind is as frustrating as trying to put toothpaste back into the tube. No human being is right all the time, but the following guidelines can help you select an advisor.

● *What is the person's reputation?* Will he or she keep confidences? (Who wants to confide in a public address system?) Do most folks salute this person's integrity and spiritual maturity? Is he or she secure enough to disagree with you, to tell the truth even when it hurts?

● *What is his or her track record as a counselor?* How did previous advice doled out by this person work out for you? Do you rate him or her highly when it comes to common sense? What do friends who have consulted with this person say? (A counselor's best advertisement is a satisfied customer.)

● *What experience does this person have with the issues at hand?* Some dilemmas require specialized feedback. If you want the Bible's perspective on a decision, your advisor needs a working knowledge of God's Word. Call on a godly relative, or a pastoral staff member in your church. If you're wrestling with changes in your adolescent's behavior, huddle with an older person who has successfully survived the parental wars.

● *How well does the person know you?* Does he or she have a handle on your strengths and weaknesses? Is he or she familiar enough with your past experiences, abilities, goals, and temperament to know how you'd react in various relational or employment contexts? If a person knows what makes you tick, he or she usually does a better job helping you sort out various alternatives.

Food for Thought

If confusion has smeared the lens of your thinking and obstructed your view of the future, hoist the four principles from the pages of this chapter and put them to work. If you do, you'll realize the truth of Proverbs 23:18: "Surely there is a future, and your hope will not be cut off."

The four insights I've put on the table don't exhaust what

Proverbs says about making choices. But it's enough for one meal. Trying to cram any more into this chapter could have the same effect on you as pigging out at an all-you-can-eat buffet: *indigestion.* What counts isn't how much Bible content you take in, but how much is converted into the energy needed for spiritual training. You've already tasted enough to exercise your options more vigorously.

Because you've sampled the smorgasbord of decision-making principles in Proverbs, it's safe to say that *your future isn't what it used to be!*

CHAPTER SIX
Cultivating Our Response-Ability

In the early 1980s, a pizza parlor owner in Allentown, Pennsylvania survived several attempts on his life. His wife placed a trip wire at the top of the stairs. When that plan failed, she hired an assailant to whack him over the head with a baseball bat. When the Lousiville Slugger left her husband with nothing worse than a headache, she had him shot—*on two separate occasions.*

While the husband slept, the first hired killer shoved a pistol against his head and pulled the trigger. After the first shooting, she drugged his chicken soup so he'd sleep soundly. The pizza maker needed more than Alka-Seltzer this time around, yet he survived. After he recuperated, his wife hired yet another gunman to shoot her groom in the chest. Miraculously, he suffered little damage. Yet more remarkable than his survival was his attitude when he discovered that his wife was behind the attacks. He forgave her on the spot. He paid her attorney fees. After she was convicted of soliciting for murder, he visited her regularly in prison.

A Hollywood director has produced a movie on their peculiar relationship titled, "I Love You to Death." It won't pose a threat to Batman's box office records, but it's an interesting story.

Few conflicts provide a plot for a movie script. Yet at any given point in time, most of us have at least one relationship that's out of kilter. Trying to get along with some folks is as frustrating as wrestling with an octopus!

If the relational atmosphere in your house, office, or church board meetings is as tense as a round of arms negotiations with the Soviets, take another excursion through the Book of Proverbs. Dotted throughout its chapters are time-tested principles for preventing or managing unhealthy forms of interpersonal conflict. It's a section of Scripture that exposes and treats life in the raw. If you apply the following advice, I can't guarantee that everyone you meet will act as neighborly as Mister Rogers. Yet God's counsel might enable you to sleep without a bullet-proof vest under your pajamas.

Trouble — with a Capital T

What is the number one manufacturer of strife between people? That's easy: *the tongue.* Two chapters in this book have already put the spotlight on the destructive and constructive power of words. Yet it's impossible to pinpoint what Proverbs says about handling conflict without referring once again to the damage caused by loose lips. We can't take a detour around principle #1: *Managing conflict requires disciplining our verbal habits and cultivating the fine art of listening.*

God doesn't beat around the bush on this issue. According to Proverbs 6:16-19, one of the "six things which the Lord hates" (v. 16) is one whose mouth "spreads strife among brothers" (v. 19). We fan the flame of hard feelings when we speak to someone in a harsh tone of voice: "A gentle answer turns away wrath, but a harsh word stirs up anger" (15:1). Or when we speak hastily without mulling over the possible consequences of our words: "There is one who speaks rashly like the thrusts of a sword" (12:18). No matter how large your halo is, you'll get angry once in a while, but a mature person taps the power of God and *thinks* about his response: "The heart of the righteous ponders how to answer" (15:28).

Another voice vice that causes relational friction is passing along damaging information about someone else. Even if the rumors are true, we'd be better off hanging an "Out of Business" sign on the door to our lips. After all, "he who spreads slander is a fool" (10:18). Whoever makes it a hobby to discuss others' faults "separates intimate friends" (16:28).

When a conversation nears the boiling point, perhaps the wisest way to cool things down is to close the lips. Lots of folks "save face" by knowing when to keep the lower half shut. "A man of understanding keeps silent" (11:12). He keeps quiet and smothers the urge to engage in a verbal sparring match because "when there are many words, transgression is unavoidable, but he who restrains his lips is wise" (10:19).

Turning off the ignition to our motormouths enables us to listen more attentively to the feelings and perspectives of others. Proverbs 18:2 employs contrast to emphasize the importance of listening: "A fool does not delight in understanding, but only in revealing his own mind." More directly, Proverbs 18:13 insists that "he who gives an answer *before he hears*, it is folly and shame to him." The Lord's emphasis on cultivating the capacity to listen reminds me of a poster I saw in a store. It read, "Please don't talk so much when I'm trying to interrupt!" The only daily exercise some of us get is "jumping to conclusions," and listening is the antidote.

A listening stance stems from a genuine desire to reconcile with the other person. Without concern for the future of the relationship, controlling the tongue is an unrealistic goal. In her book *Real Friends*, Barbra Varenhorst explains how listening and caring go hand in glove. She discusses the concept of "listening with the heart":

Heart listening can be learned, but it cannot be practiced or done mechanically. You can listen mechanically with your ears, but not with your heart. Why? Because the essence of listening with your heart is to put your whole self into trying to hear what the other is saying, because you care that much. Unless you care, you won't stop talking, resisting, or ignoring long enough to hear what is being said. You won't sacrifice your time or conscience or hear the other's feelings behind the words or twisted behaviors. If you care enough, you will learn the necessary skills, and then you will practice repeatedly, putting out the effort needed to learn to "listen with your heart."[2]

Allow me to share an excerpt from Merton and Irene Strommen's *Five Cries of Parents*. Their research-based book on family issues includes a helpful section on three types of listening mistakes which do *not* represent the "listening from the heart" that adolescents need. Avoiding these mistakes can reduce the conflicts in any relationship:

Listening with Half an Ear. This is a common form of listening within a family setting. Let us imagine a scene wherein thirteen-year-old Barb storms into the house in angry tears. It seems that her best friend, Cindy, has broken a trust. Barb told her a personal secret and made Cindy promise she would tell no one. But Cindy did tell someone, and Barb is furious. "I hate her!" she cries. "I never want to see her again!"

Barb's mother is busy. It's only a few minutes before supper and she is making a tossed salad and keeping an eye on the roast in the oven. She is sympathetic, though, and asks a few questions. But then she says briskly, "Just a minute, Barb, I have to check on the meat." She turns away and opens the oven door. "Oh, dear, it's getting overdone! Keep talking, Barb; I can hear you." Barb does try to continue, but somehow it's not easy to talk when someone isn't looking at you and is preoccupied with something else.

The mother faces Barb again. "Now as you were saying about Cindy . . . " Barb's face brightens and conversation picks up. Then suddenly the mother interrupts again. "Oh, oh, I forgot to put the broccoli on and your father will be home any minute. I'll be right back." She runs downstairs to the freezer. What has happened when she returns? Barb has gone up to her room. The mother has missed a chance to enter into a painful experience with her daughter. Moreover, this is the age when a friend's betrayal is crushing. Talking about it could have brought insight into the situation; it could have brought healing.

What can a parent do in a situation such as this? After all, the mother was legitimately busy. But if one is going to listen, one has to stop what one is doing and tune in to the other person's feelings. If possible, even at a bad time such as before supper, the mother needs to listen intently for a few minutes and then explain that this is a difficult time to talk. She and her daughter should then agree to have further conversation as soon as possible. The most important element is that the adolescent know she is being heard. Her problem is important enough to warrant her mother's time later, if not right now. Self-worth is preserved.

"Yes, But" Listening. Let us imagine the same scene between Barb and her mother. This time the mother is attentive. She hears the story, asks a few questions, then quickly launches into her "advice" treatment.

"But Barb, don't you remember I told you that if you ever want anything broadcast all over town, tell Cindy? Her mother is just like her. There are some things you're going to have to learn in life, Barb. You're too trusting—just like your father. I don't mean you should be suspicious of everyone, but you have to be smart about things like that . . ."

Barb has already left the room. Anger at Cindy is now mingled with anger at her mother. Reinforced inside her is the conviction, all too common for adolescents, that you can't tell grown-ups anything. They just scold you and tell you what you should have done.

There is a strong possibility that Barb's mother gave sound advice. After all, she has lived longer than Barb, knows her community and, no doubt, more about human nature. But she didn't give the gift of herself in listening; she merely gave advice. And she missed the opportunity to help Barb discover her own way of dealing positively with this painful experience.

"I Can Top That" Listening. In this instance, Barb's mother hears part of the story. Then she says, "That's tough, Barb, but you'll get over it. If you think this is bad, let me tell you what happened when I was your age—well, maybe a year older—I can't remember exactly what year it was. But I remember I lived at the house on 32nd Street. Anyway . . . " the mother is now very animated, thinking of the incident in her past " . . . I had a friend named Joyce. We were really close. I told her that I had a crush on a boy in our class and I swore her to secrecy and she promised. The next day when I came to biology class it was plastered all over the blackboard, 'Annie loves Jack'—Jack was the boy's name . . . "

The mother looks at Barb, whose face bears little expression. In fact, she is putting on her coat, ready to leave.

What has happened? The mother has taken all the limelight, shifted the attention to herself. She never entered into her daughter's problem.[3]

If listening is so vital to preventing and resolving conflict, we need a tool to evaluate our listening habits. Mull over the eight questions that follow, and put a check mark by the appropriate answer. As you read the questions, keep one person in mind who's important to you, but with whom you've had problems getting along lately. If your responses reveal an ear problem, ask the Lord to fit you with a "hearing aid" that will pick up more of the sound waves generated by this person's speech. Remember, this tool will only be helpful if you are honest.

1. When conversing with this person, do you struggle to keep your mind from wandering?
   Usually _____ Yes _____ No _____ Sometimes _____

2. When talking with this person, do you get beyond the facts being discussed and try to determine feelings?
   Usually _____ Yes _____ No _____ Sometimes _____

3. Do certain words, phrases, mannerisms or ideas make it more difficult for you to really hear this person?
   Usually _____ Yes _____ No _____ Sometimes _____

4. When you are talking with this person, do you really listen, or are you usually thinking of what you're going to say next?
   Usually _____ Yes _____ No _____ Sometimes _____

5. If you feel it's going to take too much time to understand something this person is trying to explain to you, do you try to change the subject or finish off that particular conversation?
   Usually _____ Yes _____ No _____ Sometimes _____

6. When this person is talking to you do you try to make him or her think you are paying attention even though you're thinking of something else?
   Usually _____ Yes _____ No _____ Sometimes _____

7. When you are listening to this person are you easily distracted by other sights and sounds?
   Usually _____ Yes _____ No _____ Sometimes _____

8. As this person talks, does your "body language" inform him or her of your disinterest? Do you keep glancing at your watch? Do your eyes wander? Do you start walking backward while pretending to listen?
   Usually _____ Yes _____ No _____ Sometimes _____

If you're currently on a collision course with an adolescent, the coach of your son's baseball team, an employer, or an office associate, turn back a few pages to the chapter titled "Open

Mouth, Insert Foot." As you review the symptoms of foot-in-mouth disease in Chapter 3 and skim the practical strategies for winning the war against wayward words, ask the Lord to show you how the material relates to the hostile relationship you're experiencing.

I'm not naive. Chances are that no more than one in twenty readers will go to the trouble of plowing the soil in chapter 3 again. Whether or not *you* follow through on this tip depends on how badly you want the relationship restored. Even if you aren't to blame for the ill will, God may want to change the other person *by first changing you.*

Behind Enemy Lines

When we're squaring off with someone we love, we're usually motivated to negotiate the differences and sign a peace treaty. But sometimes we're in conflict with folks for whom we don't give a rip. We don't give beans about the prospect of intimacy with someone we label an "enemy." I'm referring to the boss who overlooked you for a well-deserved promotion. The T-ball coach whose "winning-is-everything" philosophy takes all the fun out of baseball for your kid. The so-called "Christian businessman" who swindled you out of several thousand dollars on a project. The neighbor who acts like you're the insensitive one whenever you complain about her barking dog keeping you awake.

When you see the word *enemy,* whose face appears on the dartboard of your mind? If there's someone you loathe as much as Daffy hates duck hunting season, then Proverbs has a timely, but tough-to-swallow word for you. Heeding this counsel requires a gut check. Here's conflict-resolving insight #2: *Treat enemies better than they deserve. Trust God to avenge their mistreatment of you.*

You're probably thinking that being nice to bad folks isn't nearly as natural as the contents of a health food store. Besides, it even seems hypocritical to serve somebody you'd like to shove into the ring with Mike Tyson. God understands those feelings, yet He doesn't withdraw His advice: "If your enemy is hungry, give him food to eat; and if he is thirsty, give him water to drink; for you will heap burning coals on his head, and the Lord will reward you" (Prov. 25:21-22).

What does all this mean about "heaping burning coals" on an enemy's head? If we can't get our hands on chunks of coal, could we substitute a bucket of scalding water? *Whoa!* Before you get the idea that Proverbs is condoning torture, let's consult Chuck Swindoll for a little background on this verse. He gnaws on verse 22 like a dog on a bone, getting every bit of spiritual nourishment possible from the author's real intent:

> In ancient days, homes were heated and meals were fixed on a small portable stove, somewhat like our outside barbecue grills. Frequently, a person would run low on hot coals and would need to replenish his supply. The container was commonly carried on the head. So as the individual passed beneath second-story windows, thoughtful people who had extra hot coals in their possession would reach out of the window and place them in the container atop his head. Thanks to the thoughtful generosity of a few folks, he would arrive at the site with a pile of burning coals on his head and a ready-made fire for cooking and keeping warm. "Heaping burning coals on someone's head" came to be a popular expression for a spontaneous and courteous act one person would voluntarily do for another.[4]

Before you dismiss this warmhearted approach to enemies as an evidence of weakness, or as ivory-tower nonsense, let's see what else Proverbs says on the subject. Other verses help explain the rationale for replacing our "cold pricklies" with "warm fuzzies." Our next stop is at Proverbs 24:17. At first glance this verse seems to add to the unrealistic burden already dumped on you. "Do not rejoice when your enemy falls, and do not let your heart be glad when he stumbles." But then God adds an interesting comment: "Lest the Lord see it and be displeased, and *He turn away His anger from him*" (24:18, emphasis mine).

Zoom in on that last phrase of verse 18. It means that when we nurse a grudge or treat a foe rudely, God refuses to take His own vengeance out on the other person. When we fail to pray and release our resentment to God, we hinder the divine process and may actually prevent our enemy from experiencing the negative consequences that God had in mind for him or her. That's why Proverbs 20:22 says, "Do not say, 'I will repay evil'; wait for the Lord, and he will save you." Centuries later, Paul expanded on the same point: "Never pay back evil for evil to anyone . . . so far as it depends on you, be at peace with all men. Never take your own revenge, beloved, but leave room for the wrath of God, for it is written, 'Vengeance is mine, I will repay,' says the Lord. . . . Do not be overcome by evil, but overcome evil with good" (Rom. 12:17-19, 21).

I'm aware that convincing you to obey this "love your enemy" concept is as difficult as recruiting volunteers for the Alamo. But no matter how tough these verses are to digest, applying them is still easier than living with the harmful effects of resentment. Your only other option is a get-even attitude that, when ignored, acts like a cancerous tumor which turns a healthy body into a corpse. For your own sake, give God a green light to perform emergency surgery. If you're overwhelmed by the impossibility of sweetening your sour attitude toward someone who has hurt you, admit it to the Lord. No one has enough spirituality to resolve conflict with a foe unless God gives him an intravenous injection of power.

A Christian doctor I know would nod in agreement. His teenage son learned the hard way that our time of greatest inadequacy is the moment when God intervenes. During a mile run at a district track meet, a competitor intentionally elbowed Gary, the doctor's son, on a far turn, away from the gaze of the high school officials. The bump forced Gary off the track for a few seconds—a move that *was* seen by an official. Despite protests by Gary's coach, he was disqualified from the race—an event he had a good chance of winning.

He had trained hard for the chance to win a medal, but his hopes were dashed by a track official who couldn't verify Gary's account of the incident. Gary was hot enough under the collar to leave a sunburn on the back of his neck! He experienced an unhappy secret of existence on planet Earth: sometimes life is downright unfair! As a Christian, the incident posed a stiffer test to Gary's faith than a final exam in a Bible college. How would he react? Would he keep ranting and raving for weeks about a circumstance he couldn't change, or would he ventilate his anger in prayer and call on the Lord for help?

My friend had a long talk with his son, and that simmered Gary down a bit. Then a closed-door bout with God over the unfairness of it all threw more cold water on the fires of resentment. I'm not saying that when friends consoled him the next day at school, he muttered, "Praise the Lord, anyhow!" The disqualification irked him. Yet the conversations with his dad and with God had the effect of successful chemotherapy treatment on the tumor of revenge.

Two weeks later, Gary was one of the favorites for the mile in the State Championships. A disqualification at the district level would normally keep an athlete out of the State finals, but an official protest over the controversial district meet got Gary reinstated. Who was his chief rival in the mile run? You guessed it—Elbow Eddie.

I wish this story had a fairytale ending, like the 1924 Olympic race featuring Eric Liddell of *Chariots of Fire* fame. You know, the hero reaches the finish line first to the roar of the crowd. But Hollywood producers won't pay a dime for Gary's story. The guy who had previously shoved Gary beat him by an eyelash— this time fair and square. Gary didn't feel like double-dating with the guy nor making him his college roommate. But he did go out of his way to give the winner a congratulatory handshake.

Gary displayed something rare at the State Championships. It's called "Christianity." He decided to play by God's rulebook for relationships, rather than the world's. When my doctor friend finished telling me this story, he smiled. He was prouder than he would've been if Gary had won the race. He knew who the *real* winner was out on the track.

When Gary offered his foe a handshake, he "heaped burning coals on his head" and treated the guy better than he deserved. That kind of reaction throws ice water on the smoldering fires of conflict.

Responsible Responses

Gary's reaction to injustice reminds me of another strife-dissolving principle of Proverbs. Since it involves treating folks graciously, it's a first cousin to the previous point. But for the sake of discussion, I'll give it a spot of its own as principle #3 on the conflict-resolution list: *A surefire cure for most hostilities is forgiveness. When someone sins against us, whether he's friend or foe, we're responsible for how we respond.*

When you put Proverbs 10:12 under the microscope, the idea of "responding responsibly" comes clearly into focus. Solomon used different terms, but he was advocating the same concept: "Hatred stirs up strife, but love covers all transgressions." Later on he again saluted the value of forgiveness: "A man's discretion makes him slow to anger, and it is his glory to overlook a transgression" (19:11).

By adding a verse from the New Testament to our inventory, we discover why God's insistence on forgiveness is reasonable. A few folks in the church at Colossae had trouble getting along. (Sound familiar?) Paul echoed the counsel from Proverbs: "Put on a heart of compassion . . . forgiving each other, whoever has a complaint against anyone; just as the Lord forgave you, so also should you" (Col. 3:12-13).

Here's Paul's "bottom line": *every Christian has an experiential basis for forgiving someone who's misused him.* Everyone who has received God's forgiveness knows what it's like to be treated better than he deserves. That's why there's no excuse for failing to return the favor. God repaired our relationship with Him by modeling for us the way He wants us to treat others.

Vivian got an uninvited opportunity to put this theory to the test. Here's what she said in an interview with me:

Another woman was in love with my husband. It was hard for me to believe. And hard to live with.

One evening, after the children were asleep, Chad asked me to join him on the sofa. He dropped several love letters into my lap that Dana had written him. "What can I do?" he asked. "I've never given her reason to feel this way about me." Dana and I had been close friends for over six months. She was years younger than me, and beautiful. And she was married.

She visited our house occasionally to talk about the problems she and her husband were having. We would listen, encourage her, and try to meet her needs. On one occasion, when things were particularly bad between her and Ron, we let her stay in our guest room. Their argument had come to blows and Ron punched her several times. Dana said she sensed a love among the members of our family that she had never experienced. But none of us realized she had special feelings for Chad—until the letters arrived.

Chad had a long talk with Dana and apologized if he had done or said anything to cause her feelings. And he helped her understand that her feelings were simply an attempt to make up for the inadequacies of her own marriage. Their talk resolved the issue. Everywhere, that is, except inside of me. Despite unfailing confidence in Chad, I felt threatened by Dana's feelings. My own feelings shifted from shock to anger, and from anger to bitterness. The bitter feelings distracted me from other matters. When the children came home for lunch and rapped about school, my mind was busy thinking of ways to strike back. The tension destroyed the inner peace that had been a vital part of my personal relationship with Jesus Christ.

My depression eventually forced me into God's Word for a solution. But I have to admit that when I first began reading in Scripture, I was trying to find a solution to *Dana's* problem—not mine. I searched for ammunition I could use against her. God didn't lead me to passages that tackled Dana's problem. He guided me to passages that spoke to *my* needs.

"Don't repay evil for evil. Don't snap back at those who say unkind things about you. Instead, pray for God's help for them, for we are to be kind to others, and God will bless us for it (1 Peter 3:9, TLB).

Be kind to one another, tender-hearted, forgiving each other, just as God in Christ also has forgiven you" (Eph. 4:32).

My natural reaction was to respond to Dana opposite from the way God's Word commanded. But slowly His words convicted me and began to change my attitude. The last verse that dispelled my bitterness I found in Hebrews 12:15: "Be careful that none of you fails to respond to the grace of God, for if he does there can spring up in him a bitter spirit which can poison the lives of many others" (PH). Failing to respond to God's grace is failing to relate to others in the same manner He relates to me. I thought about scores of ways in which I had offended God, yet each time He had freely forgiven me. Concentrating on *His* forgiving nature created a climate of forgiveness in my own heart. I confessed my bitterness. I had responded to Dana's sin with sin of my own.

A week after my encounter with God's Word, Dana wrote me a letter and asked me to forgive her. I wrote back, "I forgive you." And I meant it.

When someone hits us below the belt, it's only natural to

stoop to his or her level and throw an illegal counterpunch. But nobody ever said that following Christ is a *natural* thing to do.

The three conflict-evaporating insights in this chapter don't exhaust what Scripture says about repairing broken relationships, but it's enough to digest in one serving. Come to think of it, if you energetically apply these principles, there's no guarantee you'll salvage every relationship. The other person may not choose to play the game by God's rulebook. Yet over the long haul, in your relationships you'll experience more harmony than harm. Let's review.

#1 Give your ears more exercise than your lips.

#2 Treat foes better than they deserve and trust the Lord to take care of their day in court.

#3 Don't react to sins against you by sinning in return. Forgiving others *is* possible because you've experienced the Lord's forgiveness.

CHAPTER SEVEN

How to Handle a Critic

When Chuck Swindoll writes, improprieties that have nuzzled their way into my life dash for cover. He triggers laser beams of truth that burn a hole in my most vulnerable areas. In *Living Above the Level of Mediocrity*, he mentions a characteristic that is on the endangered species list among God's servants. He discusses this characteristic in concert with three others:

> There is a fourth essential characteristic when it comes to living differently, and I warn you; it is the least popular of the four. After vision and determination and priorities, I should also mention *accountability*. People who really make an impact model this rare quality.
>
> What do I mean by accountability? *In the simplest terms, it is answering the hard questions.* Accountability includes opening one's life to a few carefully-selected, trusted, loyal confidants who speak the truth—who have the right to examine, to question, to appraise, and to give counsel.
>
> Not much has been said or written about accountability. Practically every time I've spoken on the subject, I've had people say afterwards, "I've never heard this addressed. I

don't read much about it. In fact, I have seldom even used the word."

I'm not suggesting for a moment that accountability give the general public carte blanche access to any and all areas of one's private life. I do not have in mind some legalistic tribunal where victims are ripped apart with little concern for their feelings. The purpose of the relationship . . . is to be a helpful sounding board, to guard someone from potential peril, to identify the possibility of a "blind spot," to serve in an advisory capacity, bringing perspective and wisdom where such may be lacking.[1]

Bull's-eye! Swindoll hit the target again. Accountability must mark any believer who wants his faith to grow. And as Swindoll implied, experiencing accountability in our relationships necessarily involves the fine art of *receiving* as well as *giving* criticism. When we're too servile to confront, a small irritation may turn into bitterness that ruins a relationship. In the same way, making the honor roll in the school of Christian living requires passing a course on *receiving* criticism. We need folks who are willing to shine the spotlight on dark spots in our character or behavior.

The author of Proverbs nods in agreement. One of the recurring themes in the book is the priceless value of advisors and critics. The kind of feedback Swindoll describes comes from folks whom we ask to hold us accountable. But whether we invite criticism or receive some of the unsolicited variety, what are some practical tips for responding to it? How can we ferret out the unfair criticism from the constructive feedback that we desperately need? How can we *give* criticism in a Christlike manner? Later in this chapter, we'll wrestle with these questions. But first, let's identify the different types of criticism and survey what Proverbs says on the subject.

Calling All Critics

To criticize means to evaluate, or to act as a judge. Whether a critic is evaluating art, a supervisor's competency, a new movie, or somebody's social skills at a Christmas party, he observes evidences, draws conclusions, and expresses them.

We tend to associate criticism with negative feedback. To someone who has the tendency to see the flaws in everything or everybody, we say, "Don't be so critical!" But criticism can come in a positive as well as a negative form.

You're a *positive critic* when you identify a person's strengths or accomplishments. You judge a person's performance or behavior as satisfactory, or worthy of special commendation. For instance: "I like the way you stood up for Susan. She wasn't here to defend herself." Or "I'm getting a lot out of your Sunday School class. I appreciate the hours of preparation that go into each lesson." This type of criticism is expected among Christians. Paul wrote, "Encourage one another, and build up one another up" (1 Thess. 5:11).

Yet warm fuzzies aren't the only kind of feedback we need. *Negative criticism* exposes unsatisfactory behavior or achievement. The critic spots a weakness or a mistake and shines a verbal spotlight on it.

Of course, negative criticism can be either *destructive* or *constructive*. When it's based on valid evidence, thorough analysis, concern for the other person, and when it is expressed in a loving manner, negative criticism stretches the recipient and motivates him to change. Who can strengthen a weakness or avoid a mistake of which he is unaware? Gordon MacDonald salutes the value of *constructive* negative criticism to spiritual growth:

> We all need truth-tellers, even if we don't really want them. Pass them up or avoid them, and our spiritual passion may be in great jeopardy. . . .
>
> Not many people want to *tell* the truth when it's painful, and not a lot of people want to *hear* the truth if it's painful . . . .But no one grows where truth is absent. No one is pushed *to be* and *to do* the best. When you look at this deficit from a Christian perspective, it describes a situ-

ation where men and women are never going to become all that God has made them to be. . . .

One rarely grows without a rebuke. One solid and loving rebuke is worth a hundred affirmations. Rebukes are the purifiers which keep spiritual passion clear and forceful.

I have often told the story of my special friend, Philip Armstrong, a missionary leader lost in a plane crash in Alaska. We were walking along a Japanese street when I made a derogatory comment about a mutual acquaintance. "Gordon," Armstrong immediately said, "a man of God would not say such things about another person." I was exposed and knew it. He was right. The rebuke stung, and I lived with its pain for many days afterward. . . . I hear his words every time I am about to embarrass myself with a needless comment about another person. That was a rebuke that forced me to grow.[2]

But the wrong kind of negative criticism can destroy others. If it's based on hearsay, propelled by a selfish motive, or communicated in an insensitive manner, negative opinions have the same effect on a person's fragile self-esteem that Hurricane Hugo had on the city of Charleston, South Carolina in 1989.

A wise critic will balance negative feedback with positive observations. And anyone who wants to cultivate Christlike character will welcome both types of criticism. To view God's thoughts on the subject up close, fasten your seat belts and take yet another scenic route through Proverbs.

Critical Condition

Almost every page in the Book of Proverbs contains several verses that are close kin to the subject of handling or giving criticism. An exhaustive analysis requires looking at broader topics such as one's attitude toward learning, acquiring wisdom, receiving counsel, responsiveness to authority, listening, and friendship. But I'll be selective, and we'll hoist just a few of the most relevant verses.

The first thing Proverbs does is to warn us against an I-can-do-it-myself approach to Christianity. There's no escaping the fact that believers need each other. We grow spiritually through ongoing interaction with persons who share our faith. This dependence is revealed by Solomon's emphasis on a teachable spirit in relationships:

A wise man will hear and increase in learning, and a man of understanding will acquire wise counsel (1:5).

Give instruction to a wise man, and he will be still wiser (9:9).

The way of a fool is right in his own eyes, but a wise man is he who listens to counsel (12:15).

Iron sharpens iron, so one man sharpens another (27:17).

Excessive individualism permeates Christianity in Western culture. We tend to feel that we answer only to God for our actions, when in fact God Himself devised a system of horizontal accountability among His followers. When we take an "It's-none-of-your-business!" attitude toward people who dare to rebuke us, we may be refusing God's attempt to get us back on track spiritually.

Perhaps the most blatant example of an independent spirit was offered in a *USA Today* article titled, "The All New Jessica Hahn." The former church secretary, who catapulted to notoriety after a sexual tryst with PTL evangelist Jim Bakker, posed nude for *Playboy* magazine. Yet she claims to be a follower of Christ. She said that posing nude for the magazine was "probably the best time of my life—except for when I found God."

She told the *USA Today* reporter that she decided to be photographed topless and bottomless because "I realized there really isn't anybody I have to answer to. . . . The church is for sinners *and* centerfolds."[3]

Whether or not Miss Hahn's relationship with Christ is authentic isn't for me to say, but claiming that "there really isn't anybody I have to answer to" isn't compatible with the Bible's call for accountability. Her insistence on privacy reminds me of what Charles Swindoll said on the subject:

> I have formed the habit of asking about accountability when stories of someone's spiritual defection or moral fall comes to my attention. Without fail, I ask something like, "Was _____ accountable to anyone on a regular basis? Did he or she meet with 1, 2, or 3 folks for the purpose of giving and receiving counsel, prayer, and planning?" Without exception—hear me now—without a single exception, the answer has been the same: NO! *There are dangers in too much privacy.*[4]

The need for teachers, counselors, and "sharpeners" doesn't give us the option of taking a Lone Ranger approach to following Christ. Here's one way to summarize Proverbs' first insight: "He who will learn only from himself has a fool for a teacher."

After tracking this topic through Proverbs, a second impression wedged its way into my mind. The book devotes a whopping amount of space to *receiving criticism.* God obviously realizes that we need more help with how to take criticism than with doling it out. At least nineteen different verses call for a teachable spirit in response to a critic's words. Here's a sampling:

Reprove a wise man, and he will love you" (9:8).

Whoever loves discipline loves knowledge, but he who hates reproof is stupid (12:1).

Poverty and shame will come to him who neglects discipline, but he who regards reproof will be honored (13:18).

He whose ear listens to the life-giving reproof will dwell

among the wise. He who neglects discipline despises himself, but he who listens to reproof acquires understanding (15:31-32).

A rebuke goes deeper into one who has understanding than a hundred blows into a fool (17:10).

A man who hardens his neck after much reproof will suddenly be broken beyond remedy (29:1).

Critics aren't on target every time. And they don't always come across like honor graduates from the school of social etiquette. Yet Proverbs still holds us accountable for how we respond to them. Instead of muttering, "Pardon me for living!" we're told to tune in to their sound waves. Get a load of the potentially positive results of a listening stance. Whoever is willing to learn from a critic:
- *discovers the "way of life"* (6:23)
- *gets wiser* (9:9, 15:31; 19:20; 29:15)
- *will be honored* (13:18)
- *may enjoy a better-than-ever relationship with the one who confronts* (9:8; 28:23).

Yet the other side of the coin also deserves inspection. Proverbs discloses the negative consequences of a defensive, close-minded response to critics:
- *causes poverty and shame* (13:18)
- *may result in death, physically or spiritually* (15:10)
- *such a person "will be broken beyond remedy"* (29:1)
- *hurts other people, such as parents* (29:15)
- *increases our susceptibility to sin* (5:1-14).

In Proverbs 5:1-14, Solomon warns us to avoid playing with sex outside marriage. He knew from first-hand experience that loose morals lead to regret. Such a person will eventually cry "How I have hated instruction! And my heart spurned reproof! And I have not listened to the voice of my teachers, nor inclined my ears to my instructors" (5:12-13). He implies that an openness to caring critics early in life can prevent moral erosion. "He who forsakes reproof goes astray" (10:17).

In a mince-no-words style, God also labels folks who don't cultivate a teachable spirit in response to criticism. He calls them "stupid" (12:1); foolish (10:8; 17:10); and a scoffer (9:8; 13:1).

Not as much printer's ink was used to capture God's comments on *giving criticism*, yet Proverbs does imply that caring for others sometimes takes the form of confronting them. How the ones we confront respond to us is an indication of *their* character. Whether we confront, and how we do it, is a reflection of *ours:*

Do not reprove a scoffer, lest he hate you; reprove a wise man, and he will love you (9:8).

Better is open rebuke than love that is concealed. Faithful are the wounds of a friend, but deceitful are the kisses of an enemy (27:5-6).

He who rebukes a man will afterward find more favor than he who flatters with the tongue (28:23).

The last insight on the subject of criticism acknowledges everyday reality. Proverbs admits that *not everyone responds to correction with a teachable spirit.* Though the long term effect of a confrontation *may* be a closer relationship, just the opposite could occur. Even if we're tactful, folks who are immature or insecure may resent our observation and insult us (9:7-8). A few folks whose behavior warrants our criticism will use earplugs when we speak (13:1). Others will avoid whoever is willing to shoot straight with the truth: "A scoffer does not love one who reproves him, he will not go to the wise" (15:12).

Now it's time to apply all those verses. As you read the following tips on receiving and giving criticism, think of actual encounters you've had that can serve as reference points for self-evaluation.

Responsible Responses

When an employer, coworker, spouse, or friend criticizes you, it's like sitting on a tack: if the point is on target, you're bound to feel pain.

The next time someone musters enough courage to confront you, respond in a Proverbs-like manner by applying these tips. A few of these ideas I've learned in the classroom of experience. Others I've adapted from a booklet titled *Practical Criticism: Giving It and Taking It*, by John Alexander (InterVarsity Press).

• *Pray.* Ask the Lord to cultivate within you a teachable rather than a defensive spirit. Ask for the discernment to determine what's accurate, and what's exaggerated, in the critic's observations. One of the dog-eared pages in my copy of Gordon MacDonald's *Ordering Your Private World* offers this challenging anecdote:

> Dawson Trotman, the founder of the Navigators, had a good method for handling all criticism directed at himself. No matter how unfair the criticism might seem to be, he would always take it into his prayer closet and in effect spread it before the Lord. Then he would say, "Lord, please show me the kernel of truth hidden in this criticism."[5]

• *Let the critic finish.* Even if you think his or her opinion is wacky, resist the urge to interrupt. When our egos are threatened, snapping back is almost as automatic as the reflex action that causes our eyes to blink when invaded by a foreign object. Tuck Proverbs 29:11 in between the folds of your brain: "A fool always loses his temper, but a wise man holds it back." Before you respond, ask, "Is there anything else?" Let the person know you're listening by maintaining good eye contact with him.

• *To insure that you understand the complaint, restate or paraphrase the critic's observations.* Say something like, "I want to make sure I'm hearing you right. You are saying that—." Sometimes we defend ourselves against charges that were never made. Checking for understanding can also keep you from exaggerating the complaint. If someone says you were thoughtless on one occasion, he isn't necessarily labeling you an insensitive dolt.

• *If an apology is in order, be man or woman enough to do it quickly.* Putting it off only makes it harder to say you're sorry. Remember that *truth doesn't hurt—unless it ought to!* Also realize that it's difficult for most folks to confront. Set your critic at ease by thanking him or her for caring enough to approach you.

• *If you aren't immediately convinced the critic is correct, give yourself time to mull things over with a standard reply such as, "You could be right. I'll think about what you said."* By saying this, you aren't conceding anything. Yet you are telling the critic that you're taking his or her input seriously. Such a response also keeps you from rash or thoughtless reaction. "Do you see a man who is hasty in his words? There is more hope for a fool than for him" (Prov. 29:20). Taking time to mull things over gives you time to simmer down and evaluate the criticism more objectively.

• *To help you weigh the accuracy of a criticism, follow these steps:* (1) *Consider the source.* Ponder such questions as, "Is the critic a person of integrity? Does he or she have a history of loyalty to me? Is the person gaining anything by knocking me, or is he genuinely concerned about me or somebody else I've hurt?" The more respect you have for the person, the more likely he's on target with the criticism. (2) *Consider the number of people who have offered the same criticism.* When two or more folks volunteer the same painful observation, chances are their comments should be heeded. (3) *Talk to someone whose opinion you respect, and who knows you well.* Tell this person what the critic said. Then ask: "Do you have the same impression? Has this critic exposed something I need to work on? How should I respond to him or her?"

Think of the last time you were on the receiving end of what you'd call a rebuke. When you first heard the other person's remarks, how did you feel? What did you say or do in response to the criticism? Did you later take the matter to the Lord and ask Him to show you if the criticism was just? In view of the previous suggestions for responding to a critic, what would you change about your original reaction to the incident? Applying these response tips to a past incident is a way of preparing for the next time it happens.

Caring Enough to Confront

Criticism is one thing which *isn't* always more blessed to give than to receive. Yet rebukes are often God's way of communicating His truth to people. Though we should proceed with caution, pointing out someone's weakness or mistake is often the right and loving thing to do. Especially where sin is involved in the life of a Christian we know, it's our business to intervene: "If a man should be detected in some sin," wrote Paul, "the spiritual ones among you should quietly set him back on the right path, not with any feeling of superiority but being yourselves on guard against temptation" (Gal. 6:1, PH). What follows are rules for giving *constructive* negative criticism.

• *Criticize the other person in private.* Your opinion will carry more weight if it isn't blurted out over the office intercom. The easiest thing to do is vent your negative opinions behind the other person's back. But the *Christian* thing to do is to remain silent until you speak directly to the individual. Jesus said, "If your brother wrongs you, go and have it out with him at once-*just between the two of you*" (Matt. 18:15, PH, emphasis mine).

• *When possible, write out what you plan to say.* Writing an imaginary conversation in your diary or journal can help you sort through the issue and assign correct labels to your feelings. When the uncomfortable moment of confrontation arrives, you're less likely to grope for words or chicken out. And you're more apt to speak in a sensitive tone of voice.

Sometimes it's okay to put your criticism in the form of a letter. If you're pretty sure your courage will evaporate when you're eyeball-to-eyeball with the person, or if you think the individual's defensiveness won't give you a chance to finish, jot down your feelings instead. Close the note, though, with an offer to talk things over later.

● *Be sure you have earned the right to be heard.* How long have you known the other person? Do you have a track record of loyalty to him or her? Unsolicited advice is more apt to be heeded in a warm relational climate.

● *Don't jump to conclusions about the person's motives.* Speculating about motives fogs the real issue. Keep the focus on observable behavior or attitudes. Which would you rather hear: "I feel irritated when you keep me waiting for so long." Or "You're not fooling anybody. You're just trying to get me mad by showing up late!"

● *Qualify your remarks.* Avoid terms like *never* and *always.* Put the spotlight on a specific mistake or trait. If a friend acts insensitively once, don't imply that he makes the same goof day in and day out.

● *Ask questions in a tactful way to launch a confrontation.* Questions give the recipient the benefit of the doubt, and allow him to explain his motives. This procedure insures that you have sufficient evidence on which to base the critical remarks you have planned. Which is better: "What you said about Mary was way off the wall! You must be jealous of her skills!" Or, "Why did you say those things about Mary?"

Ultimately, practicing the how-tos of giving and receiving criticism is a matter of discipleship. John Alexander explains why believers shouldn't treat the topic addressed in this chapter glibly: "God has called us to unity. We really are 'one in the Spirit' and 'one in the Lord.' By developing an ability to give and take criticism, we can more fully express that unity before God and reveal that unity before men."[6]

CHAPTER EIGHT
Living with an Executive

Crack open *Webster's New Collegiate Dictionary*, and you'll find the following definition of *influence:* "Power exerted over the minds and behavior of others. The capacity of causing an effect in indirect or intangible ways."

Men, is there a better description anywhere of the impact of *women* in our lives? Even if you're the only breadwinner in the house, don't underestimate your wife's clout. In *Ten Steps to Victory Over Depression*, Tim LaHaye illustrates the influence of the lady of the house:

> The personnel director of a large corporation who had learned the powerful influence of negativism on people explained why he selected one particular man over another for a special job assignment. I knew both men and volunteered my surprise at his selection, for I felt that the man passed over was the more effective employee. He responded, "I never hire a top echelon executive until I first meet and interview his wife. Although I am aware of the tremendous capabilities of our mutual friend, I am also conscious of the excessive griping habits to which his wife is

given. I therefore concluded that she would be a harmful, de-motivating influence on his work. I chose the other man because I judged that the margin between them would easily be bridged by the supportive role of his wife.[1]

Of course, women are increasingly earning their own executive nameplates in the corporate world. Yet the personnel director cited by LaHaye revealed keen insight. He understood that whether or not a wife and mother works outside the home, her influence on family members and her contributions to them is colossal.

God made the same point centuries before the birth of Christ. He honored wives and mothers in a twenty-two verse salute at the end of Proverbs. Traditionally, Proverbs 31:10-31 has been tabbed a "mirror for a godly woman." Females can look at this portrait and identify qualities that God wants to cultivate in their character. But there's another way to view the passage. You can regard it as a handbook on the worth of a wife and mother. The author discusses various dimensions of the woman's role, covering everything from her muscle-stretching chores to her spiritual influence. Before we delve into the passage, take a minute to read Proverbs 31:10-31 from your Bible.

Finished? If you're like me, you concluded that this exalted portrait of a wife and mother belongs in an art gallery, not in a house. "Who measures up to this ideal?" you may be thinking. "Besides, aren't the duties listed in the passage a bit prehistoric? How many moms in this day and age don the role of Ocean Pacific and make jeans and pullovers for their kids? In an era when most wives work outside the home, how many crawl out of bed before sunrise to cook French toast and sausage? Frosted Flakes or Egg McMuffins are the rule, not the exceptions."

If you're nursing these notions, I commend you. The questions indicate that you're interacting with the material. But whether or not today's woman performs all the tasks mentioned in Proverbs 31 isn't the point. Don't think the Bible is a straitjacket, condemning the female to a rigid, suffocating routine.

Whether she's a real estate agent or a full-time housewife, plants a mouth-watering garden or gets her vegetables at the supermarket, the Proverbs 31 description is as contemporary as laser surgery or nuclear arms talks. *What we're after are the character traits reflected in the household responsibilities outlined in the passage.* By itemizing the types of contributions made by this ideal woman, we'll discover the value of the more down-to-earth women in *our* lives.

May the following pages whack your thinking into high gear, and increase you appreciation for the lady of your house.

Physical Fitness

The lady depicted in Proverbs 31 didn't need a Jane Fonda workout video to help her get in shape. Her house was one big exercise spa! Note the calories burned in the following excerpts from her schedule:

> She looks for wool and flax,
> and works with her hands in delight.
> She is like merchant ships;
> she brings her food from afar.
> She rises also while it still night,
> and gives food to her household,
> and portions to her maidens.
> She considers a field and buys it;
> From her earnings she plants a vineyard (vv. 13-16).

> She stretches out her hands to the distaff,
> and her hands grasp the spindle (v. 19).

> She makes coverings for herself (v. 22).
> She makes linen garments and sells them,
> and supplies belts to the tradesmen (v. 24).

> She looks well to the ways of her household,
> and does not eat the bread of idleness (v. 27).

Shopping, cooking, sewing, gardening—it's no wonder verse 17 says that she "girds herself with strength, *and makes her arms strong.*" In the days before automobiles, microwaves, Maytag washers, and garden tillers, her routine made her the arm-wrestling champ of the family! On top of it all, the woman pictured here earned a part-time income. Maybe that's why she hired maids to help with the housework (v. 15).

Perk up your ears, and you may hear God's Spirit whisper the following questions: *What taken-for-granted physical chores does your wife perform on a regular basis? How does the diligence modeled by the Proverbs 31 woman show up in her?* Even if you're from a home where you and the kids pitch in around the house, chances are she works overtime to meet your basic needs.

Bob Peters would shout "amen!" to that remark. I read his story under one of the most eyebrow-raising headlines ever offered by my daily newspaper. The words leaped off the newsprint, grabbed me by the throat, and demanded attention: **Macho Ex-Marine Admits Failure As "Housewife."**

The United Press International feature described the sobering experience of Bob Peters, a former marine and Stanford All-America defensive end who can bench press 400 pounds. For nine months of the year, the former Palo Alto Jaycee Man of the Year was a high school football and wrestling coach. When June rolled around one year, his wife took a summer job while he stayed home with their four kids, aged 4 to 16. He signed a 70-day "motherhood" contract which spelled out his responsibilities: tutor, financial manager, arbitrator, disciplinarian, chef, recreational director, and maid, to name a few.

How did he fare? "It's an impossible task for any human being," he concluded. "I really didn't realize it was so hard. I'm in good physical condition. I'm big and strong, but since I've been doing this, I've lost 10 pounds that I didn't want to lose. It's because of the running around, getting up early and staying up late. It's folding the last load of clothes and trying to figure out where I put it all—that's kind of a trick."

Peters says he didn't come close to achieving all the goals in the contract, but at least he learned the hard way that "a mom's job is not one of viewing one soap opera after another and hosting Tupperware parties and such." Because he couldn't hack the role, Peters says the President should appoint a national commission to "promote a renaissance of respect and admiration for mothers everywhere."[2]

Peters' experiment shows if serving as a housewife and mom isn't the toughest job in the world, it ranks right up there with fighting forest fires or serving as an arbitrator for a Middle East conflict.

House Executive

A myth needing burial is that a woman's contribution to the family is limited to physical labor that any healthy person could perform. Proverbs' portrait shows a woman with a highly-developed brain as well as steel-plated biceps. Her role requires managerial ability that would make any Fortune 500 company look twice at her resumé. Taking care of a family is like running a small business. And in most homes, even where Dad is Chairman of the Board, most administrative duties are delegated to you-know-who.

Look closer at the Proverbs 31 portrait, and you'll see the following evidence of managerial know-how:

• *Delegation.* The size of her house and family made it necessary to hire outside help. Her early-morning duties included planning the schedules of her employees. The "portions" given to her maidens in verse 15 refers to prescribed tasks. To keep a work crew happy and productive takes more administrative genius than you think.

• *Money Management.* She budgeted money for the food and fabric needed to sustain the family (vv. 13-14). With leftover fabrics, she made garments to display at weekend garage sales (v. 24). That required the expertise of an accountant: figuring out profit margins, sale prices, and so forth. She invested her earnings in real estate, purchasing a garden plot as a way to help satisfy the appetites of family members (v. 16). Planning was an integral part of her agenda. She did an annual inventory of the kids' and her husband's closets, anticipated needs for winter wardrobes, then made the clothes they'd need months in advance (v. 21).

• *Wise Counsel.* The writer of Proverbs 31 applauds the wisdom of a woman's words: "She opens her mouth in *wisdom,*" he asserts (v. 26). With few exceptions, God has given women a special ability to think practically and to employ wisdom in specific situations that crop up. That wisdom enables them to make smart managerial decisions, and to offer sound advice when they're consulted over a problem.

A man I know asked his wife to help pick out a new family car. As a salesman escorted them along a row of new models, the woman kept wanting to see the trunk of each car. After several trunk inspections, the frustrated salesman blurted, "Lady, most folks inspect the engine rather than the trunk!"

Her reply? "I assume any new engine will run okay for a few years. But you can't determine the size of the trunk without looking. We travel a lot, and luggage always ends up under our feet and behind our heads. So just keep opening the trunk, please."

On a scale of 1–10, I don't know how you'd rank your wife's administrative skill. The passage in Proverbs is merely demonstrating that managing a household takes brain as well as brawn. Even women who aren't executive material fulfill more managerial functions than we give them credit for. Keeping your business records in the computer and an extra jar of peanut butter in the cupboard requires administrative know-how.

Influence Outside the Home

The profile in Proverbs 31 suggests that a woman's primary responsibility is to her husband and kids. Yet you get the impression that the lady described here wasn't a prisoner of her four walls. Her gifts and abilities weren't kept under lock and key. Far from being a social invalid, she supplemented her substantial commitment to the family with dimensions of fulfillment outside the house.

We've already discussed how she used her proficiency as a tailor to supplement her husband's income (v. 24). And we've seen how she had the freedom to invest her earnings as she saw fit (v. 16). But the scope of her influence widens even more in verse 20: "She extends her hand to the poor; and she stretches out her hands to the needy." One result of her efficient family management and relief work in the community was the lofty reputation of her husband. Her contributions increased the respect peers had for him (v. 23). They realized how smart he was for marrying her!

If it weren't for the contributions of moms and housewives, the fabric of society would unravel. In what ways does your wife's scope of influence extend beyond the four walls of your house? Does she work for money in order to help save for your children's college tuition? Does she teach a rowdy gang of kids week after week in Sunday School or write letters of encouragement to hurting people? Does she cook for the neighbors when the lady of the house is ill? Does she visit folks in the hospital or share cookies with families who can't afford chocolate chips? If you answer "yes" to even one question of that sort, she probably deserves more kudos than she gets.

Spiritual Savvy

What motivates the Proverbs 31 woman to serve her family and community selflessly? *Her close bond with the Lord!* The wisdom and diligence previously cited sprout from spiritual soil that's regularly cultivated.

She's called an "excellent" wife in verse 10. That adjective literally means "strong"—strong in character. According to verse 30, her most praiseworthy trait is a reverence for God: "Charm is deceitful and beauty is vain, but a woman who fears the Lord, she shall be praised." More important than her social standing or appointments with her hairdresser is nurturing her relationship with the Lord.

The spiritual zeal of such a God-fearing woman is contagious. John Wesley was founder of the Methodist Church in the 18th century. His brother Charles wrote hundreds of Christian hymns, some of them printed in the song book you hold every Sunday. What accounted for their immeasurable contributions to church history? A devout mother. Susanna Wesley gave birth to seventeen kids, yet she locked herself in her room for one hour every day just to pray for them.

Maybe your wife doesn't reserve a prayer closet for sixty minutes a day, but odds are that her spiritual savvy improves the atmosphere in your home. What evidences of a heart for God do you see in her? How has she invested in *your* spiritual development? What has she done to encourage your children's spiritual walk? Have you ever thanked her for the prayers she's said on your behalf? If she isn't in close touch with God, how can you encourage her spiritual resurgence? If she isn't a Christian, do you pray regularly for her salvation? Prayer is an acceptable way to rebel against the status quo in any unbeliever's life.

Monumental Praise

The person who painted this female portrait in chapter 31 put a clincher on it in verses 28-29: "Her children rise up and bless her; her husband also, he praises her, saying, 'Many daughters have done nobly, but you excel them all.' "

When it comes to gratitude, does your spouse get the short end of the stick? Few people need voice lessons to sing their own praises, but to compliment the work and character of others is a different matter. The verses we read poke a long index finger into our chest and call for expressions of appreciation on our part.

The majestic Statue of Liberty towers above the entrance to New York Harbor, a symbol of the freedom we enjoy here in America. It was a gift to the United States from the French government. A famous sculptor named Bartholdi devoted twenty years to producing the statue, even investing most of his own fortune to help the French government meet expenses of the project. From the start, Bartholdi looked for a model whose form and features he could reproduce as "Lady Liberty." After examining a list of famous and heroic women, he selected the model: *his own mother!*

You can train your kids to "raise a monument" to their mother by helping them find creative ways to express appreciation for her contributions. One dad I know helped his teenage son write the following poem when mom was bedridden with an illness:

Taken for Granted

Some moms get taken out to dinner
    at a restaurant fit for a queen.
Then they're taken where waists get thinner—
    to a spa that can make then lean.
Others get taken on a second honeymoon,
    or a cruise to a place enchanted.
But mom's like you, more often than not,
    just get *taken for granted!*

If neither you nor the kids can make words rhyme, look for other ways to build a monument in her honor. Does one of the following ideas grab you?

• *Empty Envelope.* Lick a stamp and put it in the corner of a letter envelope. Write her name and address on the envelope. Go ahead and seal the envelope. Yea, I know it's empty. Just follow directions. On the *back* of the envelope jot down these words: "Inside this envelope you'll discover what my life would be without you." Then mail it.

• *First-Class Gratitude.* This time put a letter in the envelope. Start the note with the words, *I thank God for you because* ———————————————. Think of specific ways to fill in the blank.

• *Sumptuous Spread.* Get your kids in on this one. Reserve a table at her favorite restaurant. During the meal, each of you take turns telling one thing you appreciate about her. (One more thing. Don't give her the check!)

• *Surprise Symbol.* Go to a Christian bookstore or a craft shop and pick out a wall plaque or other decorative item for the house. Tell her it's a concrete way of thanking her for her contributions to the family. Every time she sees it, she'll realize that her work isn't taken for granted.

Without draining your bank account or slicing twenty years off your life, you and your children can build your own version of the Statue of Liberty in honor of the lady in your house!

CHAPTER NINE
Earthly Minded

If you like original dishes, here's one for you:

A friend of mine ate dog food one evening. No, he wasn't at a fraternity initiation or a hobo party . . . he was actually at an elegant student reception in a physician's home near Miami. The dog food was served on delicate little crackers with a wedge of imported cheese, bacon chips, an olive, and a sliver of pimento on top. That's right, friends and neighbors, it was hors d'oeuvres a la Alpo.

The hostess is a first-class nut! You gotta know her to appreciate the story. She had just graduated from a gourmet cooking course, and so she decided it was time to put her skill to the ultimate test. Did she ever! After doctoring up those miserable morsels and putting them on a couple of silver trays, with a sly grin she watched them disappear. One guy (my friend) couldn't get enough. He kept coming back for more. I don't recall how they broke the news to him . . . but when he found out the truth, he probably barked and bit her on the leg! He certainly must have gagged a little.[1]

The hostess skillfully illustrated the fine art of deception. She tricked her guests into thinking they were swallowing expensive snack food concocted in her upper-class kitchen. Instead, she made her pet cocker spaniel howling mad by robbing him of his supper. After telling this story, Chuck Swindoll goes on to discuss the matter of deception:

> If you want to make a counterfeit dollar bill, you don't use yellow construction paper, cut it in the shape of a triangle, put the Lone Ranger's picture in the center, and stamp "3" on each corner. That deceives nobody. Deception comes in a *convincing* fashion, wearing the garb of authenticity, supported by the credentials of intelligence, popularity, and even a touch of class. By the millions, gullible gluttons are duped into swallowing lies, thinking all the while they are digesting the truth. In reality they are underscoring the well-worn words of Phineas Taylor Barnum: *"There's a sucker born every minute."*[2]

This is the first of two chapters which discuss one of the most delicious deceptions ever served up by Satan. He expertly disguises the truth and shoves this delectable morsel into the minds of millions: *The key to happiness is "having."* He says that *the more money and material things we accumulate, the more meaningful life will be.* At first what he offers satisfies the taste buds. The more we digest his philosophy, though, the more sick we become. Anyone who keeps picking from Satan's platter eventually gags on the contents. For no matter how you decorate it, Alpo is *still* dog food!

God's Word is chock-full of teaching on the subject of money and values. In his tape series "Mastery of Materialism," John MacArthur says, "Sixteen out of thirty-eight of Christ's parables deal with money. More is said in the New Testament about money than heaven and hell combined. Five times more is said about money than prayer, and where there are five hundred plus verses on both prayer and faith, there are over two thousand

verses dealing with money and possessions."[3] It's obvious that
God wants to combat Satan's deception in this area. Perhaps
Proverbs served as inspiration for New Testament authors, for
its pages are teeming with comments about our attitude toward
possessions.

As you examine Proverbs' teaching on this topic, you won't
find even a hint that wealth is wrong. No one gets spiritual
brownie points just because he's poor. As a matter of fact,
Proverbs applauds diligence on the job, and salutes folks who
are rewarded because they work hard. For instance, Proverbs
10:4 says, "Poor is he who works with a negligent hand, but the
hand of the diligent makes rich." Proverbs 13:11 is one of several other verses which reiterate the same point: "Wealth obtained by fraud dwindles, but the one who gathers by labor
increases it." But the Book of Proverbs does expose the foolish-
ness of banking too much on riches and working solely for
selfish reasons. And it suggests that a passion for material things
siphons off our devotion to God and hinders our usefulness to
Him.

This chapter and the next chapter survey Proverbs' teaching
on material values and tackle the following questions: To what
extent are adults preoccupied with material things? What type
of things are more valuable and desirable than material possessions? How does materialism show up in a person's life? On
what basis do we evaluate our attitude toward money and our
use of it? How can we tell if money is our master or our servant?
You won't find God's truth served on a silver platter. Yet in the
long run, digesting it is much better for your health than de-
vouring a delicacy. And even if your taste buds rebel against
God's Word at first, it's easier to stomach than the tastiest items
off Satan's menu.

Is Money Our Master?
Before delving into Proverbs, let's define materialism and focus
on some of the evidence that materialism is threatening our
devotion to God. According to *Webster's Third New International*

Dictionary, materialism is "a preoccupation with, or tendency to seek after or stress material rather than spiritual things." Writer Steve Thurman expands this definition:

> A materialist is someone who is *preoccupied* with the things of this world, cares *too much* for the things that can be purchased, spends his day dreaming only of the next acquisition. And he is frustrated if he can't get what he wants when he wants to have it.
>
> For the materialist, life is a *preoccupation* with jewelry, or landscaping, or remodeling the home, or trips abroad, or nice cars, or a business deal. Life revolves around these things. He is obsessed with the "stuff" of life.[4]

Whenever Satan whispers that cash and credit cards are avenues to fulfillment, a lot of us are cupping our ears to listen. A lot of us are literally buying into the philosophy of a bumper sticker I spotted recently: "The man who dies with the most toys wins." Zoom the lens of your mind in on the following trends:

● A recent survey of more than 200,000 entering freshmen at 590 colleges disclosed disturbing information. They're growing more materialistic, while at the same time becoming less concerned about non-material values. A record 76 percent listed financial prosperity as an "essential" or "very important" life goal. Yet only 39 percent of the same group listed "developing a meaningful philosophy of life" as important. That's in stark contrast to a similar survey of college freshmen taken twenty years ago. At that time, 83 percent listed "a meaningful philosophy of life" as a key goal. Alexander Astin, director of the more recent survey, concludes, "Our data show that greed is alive and well!" He says the trend toward materialism has been rising steadily in recent years. "Obviously we're seeing something very profound in society," he admits.[5]

Our regard for the perspective of Proverbs 23:4-5 is waning: "Do not weary yourself to gain wealth, cease from your consideration of it. When you set your eyes on it, it is gone. For wealth certainly makes itself wings, like an eagle that flies toward the heavens."

● A group called Empty Tomb, Inc. studied the giving patterns in 31 Christian denominations. Although average income after taxes rose 31 percent between 1968 and 1985, per-member church giving dropped almost 9 percent. According to Tom Sine, in a book title *Why Settle For More and Miss the Best?*, Christians under the age of 35 give significantly less to Christian organizations than do those over 35—despite evidence that young adults are better off than they've ever been. "As this younger population ages," writes Sine, "the economic base of all kinds of Christian enterprises will be in trouble if we don't teach our young people to look beyond themselves."[6]

● Financial insecurity is considered the chief threat to American family life, with over half (56 percent) citing economic problems as their biggest concern. The leading cause of financial worry is inadequate family resources (30 percent), followed by the high cost of living (11 percent), unemployment (6 percent), taxes (5 percent), and the safety of their investments (4 percent). Financial problems worry more women (61 percent) than men (51 percent).[7]

● In a summary of a study conducted by his magazine, the managing editor of *Money* magazine concluded that money has become the number-one obsession of Americans. "Money has become the new sex in this country," he said. In a similar vein, *Newsweek* magazine described Americans as having achieved a new plane of consciousness called "transcendental acquisition."[8]

● The proliferation of state lotteries reinforces the point made by *Money* and *Newsweek* magazines. Back in April 1989, the "pot" in Pennsylvania's Super 7 Lottery swelled to a $100 million prize—at the time a record amount. Out-of-staters purchased tickets over the phone by credit card—a minimum of 50 tickets for $100, plus a $10 fee for overnight delivery. Other rainbow chasers flew to Greater Pittsburgh International Airport from as far away as California just to buy lottery tickets at two machines in the main terminal. A 30-year-old Houston lady bought a $796 round-trip ticket to Pittsburgh because "I had a vision a year ago that I won the largest jackpot in lottery history. I missed Illinois, I missed Florida, so this is my turn. I'm about to faint, I'm so nervous," she said. If she won, she planned to divorce her husband and claim all the jackpot for herself. The $300 she spent for tickets, though, was peanuts compared to the $1,700 shelled out by a California traveler.

Their lotto fever probably made them seriously ill, though, when the winner was announced. An individual's odds of winning was 1 in 9.6 million. If you had purchased a lottery ticket for this Pennsylvania jackpot, you'd have a better chance of having both your main and backup parachutes fail to open: 1 in 9 million. Or being struck by lightning: 1 in 609,944.[9]

Lots of Christians who shun the lottery still get trapped in the "happiness is having" mindset. Steve Thurman's story about a remorseful Texan is more typical than we want to admit:

A few years ago I was sitting in my office in Dallas, and a man wandered in and sat down. He was nervous and embarrassed, shaking a bit. He had come in for one purpose: to sit in my office and cry, and tell me why.

"I'm a Christian," he said. "I love the Lord. I had a beautiful wife who loves the Lord. I had a good job and a good income, enough to take care of my family. We were involved in the church.

"But the money was never enough. I chased it and chased it and chased more of it. I traveled when I didn't have to travel. I had to succeed, I had to make more, I had to prove myself, and I wanted more *money*.

"It didn't take long before our marriage was kaput. My wife left me. I rarely see my children anymore, and I've got an emptiness inside that I can't even describe."[10]

If only he could have learned from the words of John D. Rockefeller. Someone asked him, "How much money is enough?" "Just a little more," he replied. Proverbs 28:19 is as timely today as when a wise man originally penned it: "He who tills his land will have plenty of food, but he who follows empty pursuits will have poverty in plenty."

Where do *you* fit into the previously cited trends and statistics? Are you discovering that *the less you have to live for, the more you need to live on?*

The Heart of the Problem

In the schoolroom of experience, I've learned that the problem of earthly-mindedness plagues folks at *all* income levels. As a Bible college professor, I've never earned what most Westerners would call an enviable salary. To my chagrin, I used to think that anyone who enjoyed economic perks beyond my reach was a slave to materialism. I assumed they neglected weightier priorities in order to enjoy their higher standard of living. How naive—and *wrong*—I was. Some of the most generous, heavenly minded folks I know are physicians, lawyers, and businessmen who invest more in God's work than they ever will in the stock market.

Ironically, *I* was the materially-minded person. God's X-ray vision penetrated my heart and revealed my envy of others' economic status. Dissatisfaction with my status quo is every bit as materialistic as neglecting church and family matters for the sake of a fatter paycheck.

In a novel titled *The Lady's Confession*, George MacDonald helped me see that materialism is a matter of the heart, not net worth. He shared his views on the subject through the lips of Thomas Wingfold, a curate in the Church of England. The following excerpt from one of the curate's sermons exposes ways a materialistic heart shows up in our actions and attitudes. I'll warn you in advance—these words jabbed me into submission, and I collapsed on the canvas for a ten count.

"You cannot serve God and mammon." A few stirred uneasily at the authority in his voice.

Who said this?

Is he not the Lord by whose name you are called, in whose name this church was built, and who will at last judge every one of us? And yet how many of you are trying your hardest to do the very thing your Master tells you is impossible? I appeal to your own conscience. Are you not striving to serve God *and* mammon?

Do you say to yourselves that it cannot be? Surely if a man strove hard to serve both God and mammon, he would soon see that it was impossible. It is not easy to serve God, but it is easy to serve wealth. Surely the incompatibility of the two endeavors must quickly become apparent. But the fact is there is no strife in your lives. But for God you do not even ask yourselves the question whether or not you are serving Him at all.

Some of you are at this very moment indignant that I call you materialistic. Those of you who are assured that God knows you are His servants know also that I do not mean you. Therefore, those who are indignant at being called the servants of mammon are so because they are indeed such.

When a man talks of the joys of making money, or boasting of number one, meaning himself, then he is a servant of mammon. If when you make a bargain you think only of yourself and your own gain, you are a servant of mammon. If in the church you would say to the rich man, "Sit here in a good place," and to the poor man, "Stand there," you are a mammon server. If you favor the company of the popular and those whom men call well-to-do, then you are serving mammon and not God. If your hope of well-being in times to come rests upon your houses or lands or business or savings, and not upon the living God, whether you are friendly and kind or a churl whom no one loves, you are equally a server of mammon. If the loss of your goods would take from you the joy of life, then you serve mammon. If with your words you confess that God is the only good, and yet you live as if He had sent you into the world to make yourself rich before you die; if it will add a pang to the pains of your death to think that you have to leave your fair house, your trees, your horses, your shop, your books all behind you, then you are a server of mammon and far truer to your real master than he will prove to you. . . . If you are poor, then don't mourn over your purse when it is empty. He who desires more than God wills him to have, he also is a servant of mammon, for he trusts in what God has made and not in God Himself. He who laments what God has taken from him, he is a servant of mammon. He who cannot pray because of the worldly cares pressing in on him is a servant of mammon.[11]

As MacDonald clearly points out, materialism can come in the form of wanting what we don't have, as well as hoarding what we do have.

If an old-fashioned work ethic oozes from your pores, and God has given you the wits to earn cash without slacking off on family priorities and ministry involvement, I'm not erecting a stop sign to your lifestyle. But I *am* putting up a caution light. It doesn't require a crystal ball to see that a love affair with money eventually hardens our hearts toward God and other people. I just don't want you to be hoodwinked by the off-the-wall philosophy that equates *things* with *joy*.

As you read what Proverbs says on the subject, remember that only God's Spirit has a right to push your guilt button. Let the Holy Spirit question you as you read.

God's Standards of Wealth

Seven words capture the main point Proverbs makes on the subject of material resources: *money has never yet made anyone rich.* At least, not in God's economy. Folks who go bonkers over bank accounts and allow things to eclipse God's Son from their eyes miss out on more valuable assets. Solomon, who lived to regret a self-indulgent lifestyle (see Chapter 2), finally admitted that "it is *the blessing of the Lord* that makes rich" (Prov. 10:22). And he wasn't referring primarily to material blessings.

Why does the Bible frequently warn us about the magnetic pull of a "more" mentality? Because material investments pale in comparison to the worth of spiritual stock. Here are some of the things God puts a higher price tag on than a BMW and a house in the suburbs:

• *A good name.* "A good name is to be more desired than great riches, favor is better than silver and gold" (Prov. 22:1). This isn't a reference to popularity or social standing. These words are talking about the rare and precious commodity of Christian character. When folks see or hear your name, what pops into their minds? Is your name synonymous with integrity? Will your children inherit godliness along with your property? "A righteous man who walks in his integrity—how blessed are his sons after him" (Prov. 20:7).

• *Wisdom.* "How blessed is the man who finds wisdom," wrote Solomon. "For its profit is better than the profit of silver, and its gain than fine gold" (Prov. 3:13-14). In Proverbs 8:11 he added, "Wisdom is better than jewels; and all desirable things cannot compare with her." Solomon was referring to the kind of discernment and common sense that comes only from God. "The fear of the Lord is the beginning of wisdom, and the knowledge of the Holy One is understanding" (Prov. 9:10). Or stuff the following words into the creases of your mind: "The Lord gives wisdom; from His mouth come knowledge and understanding. He stores up sound wisdom for the upright" (2:6-7).

• *Truthfulness.* Most folks get their cash the old-fashioned way: they *earn* it! But fudging on integrity in order to make a buck is still more common than Lincoln pennies. About $100 billion a year is lost through tax cheating. And a survey conducted for *U.S. News and World Report* found that one-third of adults aged 18-29 feel "there are some circumstances in which stealing from an employer is justified."[12]

Our Lord says, "It is better to be a poor man than a liar"

(Prov. 19:22). Besides, spending money obtained dishonestly will haunt people in the long run: "The getting of treasures by a lying tongue is a fleeting vapor, the pursuit of death" (Prov. 21:6). If God doesn't mete out their punishment in the here and now, frauds will get their just due when Jesus returns to earth: "Riches do not profit in the day of wrath, but righteousness delivers from death" (Prov. 11:4).

● *Lips of Knowledge.* Teaching others—especially when it comes to sharing God's truth—is a wiser investment than faceted emeralds: "There is gold, and an abundance of jewels; but the lips of knowledge are a more precious thing" (Prov. 20:15). Whenever the glitter of a gemstone tantalizes my eyes, that verse puts my Bible teacher's salary in proper perspective. Does the pursuit of extra money siphon off time and energy you need to teach a Sunday School class? To build a relationship with a non-Christian neighbor as a context for sharing the Gospel? Those are the type of questions the Holy Spirit asks me on a regular basis.

● *Harmonious relationships.* Graze on the truth of Proverbs 15:16-17: "Better is a little with the fear of the Lord, than great treasure and turmoil with it. Better is a dish of vegetables where love is, than a fattened ox and hatred with it." I don't know about you, but I'd rather eke out a living than go bankrupt in my relationships. Who can put a price tag on the gift of other people's love or on a sense of belonging to somebody else?

Gold Rush

None of the verses you've read in this chapter condemn money. God merely wants us to see its relative importance in comparison to other treasures. So long as they don't possess us, possessions aren't a problem. God's warning is reserved for folks who worship at the shrine of wealth, who bracket off the financial area of their lives from divine influence. When it comes to growing dollar bills, having a green thumb isn't a crime. Yet "he who *trusts* in his riches will fall" (Prov. 11:28, emphasis mine).

Yussif, a professional wrestler nicknamed the "Terrible Turk," needed that reminder two generations ago. He literally demonstrated the truth of Proverbs 11:28. The 350-pound behemoth grabbed athletic glory all over Europe and the United States. When in a match against the United States' best wrestler, Yussif tossed the American champ across the ring like a teddy bear, then pinned him. The Terrible Turk demanded the $5,000 winner's purse in gold coins. When he boarded the ship back to Europe, he crammed the gold coins into his huge belt. During the voyage, the ship began to sink. The wrestler went over the side with his bulging belt full of gold still strapped to his enormous waist. The added weight kept him from staying afloat until the lifeboats could arrive. Yussif and his gold plunged straight to the bottom of the Atlantic. Neither before or since that day has the value of gold ever sunk so fast![13]

If God has plopped you into a job that earns six figures or you have a knack for choosing smart investments, you don't owe anyone an apology. Not as long as you keep material things in proper perspective, and make it a habit to invest in those less tangible commodities deemed more precious by God.

Hundreds of years after the proverbs were collected, Paul echoed Solomon's point and elevated the worth of character and relationships over material resources:

> But godliness actually is a means of great gain, when accompanied by contentment. For we have brought nothing into the world, so we cannot take anything out of it either. . . . But those who want to get rich fall into temptation and a snare and many foolish and harmful desires which plunge men into ruin and destruction. For the love of money is a root of all sorts of evil, and some by longing for it have wandered away from the faith, and pierced themselves with many a pang (1 Tim. 6:6-7, 9-11).

The Terrible Turk would have scoffed at those verses. His greed tossed him out of the ring for good.

CHAPTER TEN
Releasing
Your Resources

The *Oakland Tribune* recently ran a "How Cheap Are You?" contest. The newspaper asked readers to submit their money-saving ideas. The responses revealed skinflints in the categories of gross, tacky, unbelievable, incredible, and downright dishonest.

A retired welder won top tightwad honors. To save coins, he separates two-ply toilet paper. Among the gross, a Berkeley couple said they save dental floss on a bathroom hook so it can be reused. Another reader claims he refreezes used ice cubes.

As for tacky, one couple collects two-for-one coupons to restaurants, then invites another couple. "We make them pay for their half, and we dine free," they reported. In the unbelievable category, another reader wrote: "I regulate my bodily functions so that I go to the bathroom only during working hours. It saves on water, tissue, and time at home. I can spend my hours at home doing something constructive, like cutting off expiration dates on coupons."

Another submission came from a man in El Cerrito. When his vacuum bag fills, he cuts one end, empties it, and sews it up for reuse. "Not only does it save bags, but sometimes I find a penny in the dust," he asserted. But I believe the award should have gone to the man who keeps a paper bag in his car with "Out of Order" printed on it. He places the bag on parking meters next to his car!¹

Save all the coupons, ice cubes, and dental floss you want. God doesn't mind. But He *doesn't* want such a miserly attitude seeping over into your relationship with Him or with other folks. Whenever you creatively cut corners in order to conserve funds, He wants others, as well as yourself, to benefit from it.

The previous chapter introduced you to the subject of materialism. You saw evidence that folks' appetite for money is escalating. And you discovered that it is good character—not ownership of things—that makes a person wealthy in God's economy. On the pages that follow, you will notice how Proverbs expands its coverage of the topic by disclosing two unselfish ways to use your earnings.

Gaining Through Giving

Proverbs unveils an unmistakable insight: *one reason God endows you with money-making ability is to give you a means of helping less fortunate people.*

How we treat the poor on planet earth is a barometer of our affection for God. Note how the Lord identifies with the needy:

He who mocks the poor reproaches his Maker (Prov. 17:5).

He who oppresses the poor reproaches his Maker, but he who is gracious to the needy honors Him (Prov. 14:31).

He who is gracious to a poor man lends to the Lord (Prov. 19:17).

Jesus saluted Proverbs' emphasis on divine identification with the poor. After encouraging His followers to feed the hungry, clothe the naked, and visit the sick and imprisoned, He said,

"To the extent that you did it to one of these brothers of Mine, you did it to Me" (Matt. 25:40).

Various proverbs also reveal the benefits of an open-handed as opposed to a tight-fisted policy. When we share with others instead of squirreling away things solely for our own consumption, look how God responds:

The generous man will be prosperous (11:25).

He who gives to the poor will never want, but he who shuts his eyes will have many curses (28:27).

He who is generous will be blessed, for he gives some of his food to the poor (22:9).

Happy is he who is gracious to the poor (14:21).

God isn't guaranteeing us a beachfront condo or early retirement. But He does say He'll take care of unselfish people. And ironically, He insists that the gratification of giving beats the giddiness of receiving anytime. The equation of joy and giving seems as foreign to some of us as the island of Sri Lanka. But check it out. Few penny-pinchers stay happy for very long. I read about a billionaire oil magnate who couldn't enjoy his wealth. He was so uptight about losing it that he installed a pay phone in his mansion for overnight guests. To top it all off, he saved on electricity by replacing all 100-watt light bulbs in his house with the 60-watt variety. He died wealthier, all right. And miserable.

We can't drive a wedge between Christianity and meeting needs of hurting people. Verses like Proverbs 29:7 won't let us: "The righteous is concerned for the rights of the poor, the wicked does not understand such concern."

Your involvement with the poor, whether in your local community or overseas, can take many forms. If they're in good condition, donate clothes you've outgrown to the Salvation

Army or some other local relief agency. Why clutter your closet in anticipation of a garage sale when scores of families in your area can't even afford a trip to K-Mart? You could also take a summer missions trip to a poverty-stricken part of the world. If nothing else, the exposure will prove that you're materially better off than you think. It's eye-opening to compare yourself with the rest of the world instead of with business associates who live in an adjacent subdivision. Many local churches and denominational headquarters sponsor short-term mission trips for laymen. If you're open to such a venture, chat with your pastor about the possibilities.

Numerous Christian agencies exist to help channel funds and supplies to needy folks all over the world. One of the best known is World Vision, a non-profit agency that provides emergency aid, furthers evangelism, and increases public awareness of poverty around the globe. Drop them a line. Ask them to increase your awareness of the needs of the poor and to inform you of realistic ways you can pitch in and help. You won't have to wait long for a reply.

In the previous chapter, I emphasized that materialism is a matter of the heart, not income level. And I explained how the Lord had exposed my own tendency to envy the wealthy and to grasp things tightly. Recently, He put the spotlight on my innate selfishness through a closetful of clothes our two boys had outgrown. After rummaging through a ten-year span of sizes, we created a stack of top-quality jeans, shirts, and sweaters worth hundreds of dollars—even at garage sale prices.

Having started a coin-collecting hobby, I fantasized about the silver dollars and walking Liberty halves I could purchase with the proceeds. The anticipated financial windfall made the hours devoted to sorting and pricing the items for our garage sale seem like minutes.

Ironically, that was the week I began collecting data from Proverbs for these chapters on money. You guessed it: verses highlighting God's concern for the needy pricked my conscience. His Spirit reminded me of several international families at our Bible college whose quiver included young boys. The heads of these homes were full-time students training for vocational ministry. They often ran out of money before they ran out of month. The verses that scuttled my garage-sale plans were Proverbs 3:27-28: "Do not withhold good from those to whom it is due, when it is in your power to do it. Do not say to your neighbor, 'Go, and come back, and tomorrow I will give it,' when you have it with you."

I argued with the Holy Spirit for a couple days but finally waved a white flag and distributed the clothes to these families. My reluctance was transformed into joy when I saw the gratitude of the parents and kids. They thought Christmas had arrived several months early.

We've heard all our lives that it's more blessed to give than to receive. Yet it's clear that most of us are willing to let the other fellow have the blessing! Perhaps the following poem will jar our thinking and spur us to action:

I was hungry
And you formed a humanities club
And discussed my hunger.
Thank you.

I was in prison
and you crept off quietly
and prayed for my release.

I was naked
and in your mind you debated
the morality of my appearance.

I was sick
and you knelt
and thanked God for your health.

I was lonely

and you left me alone to pray for me.
You seem so holy,
So close to God, but

I'm still very hungry and lonely and cold.
So where have your prayers gone?
What does it profit a man
To page through his book of prayers
When the rest of the world is
Crying for his help?[2]

At least now you know what to do with all the money you save on two-ply toilet paper, used dental floss, leftover ice cubes, and surgically repaired vacuum-cleaner bags.

God Is My Banker

Chuck Swindoll writes more books in a year than some folks read in a lifetime. In a hefty hardback titled *Living Above the Level of Mediocrity*, he tells a sobering story:

I have a close friend in the ministry who traveled across the country for a week of meetings. The only problem was, his baggage didn't make it. As I recall, the bags went to Berlin! He really needed a couple of suits. So he went down to the local thrift shop and was pleased to find a row of suits. When he told the guy, "I'd like to get a couple of suits," the salesman said, "Good, we've got several. But you need to know that they came from the local mortuary. They've all been cleaned and pressed, but they were used on stiffs. Not a thing wrong with them, I just didn't want that to bother you." My friend said, "No, that's fine. That's okay." So he hurriedly tried some on and bought a couple for about twenty-five bucks apiece. Great deal!

When he got back to his room, he began to get dressed for the evening's meeting. As he put one on, to his surprise there were no pockets. Both sides were all sewed up!

Though surprised, he thought, "Why of course! Stiffs don't carry stuff with 'em when they depart!" The suits looked as if they had pockets, but they were just flaps on the coat. My friend told me later, "I spent all week trying to stick my hands in my pockets. Wound up having to hang my keys on my belt!" The minister was reminded all week long that life is temporal.[3]

That anecdote reminds me of another major observation about money offered by Proverbs: *When evaluated from an eternal perspective, making material wealth our main objective in life is foolish. Only the resources we invest in God's work reap guaranteed dividends.*

Our years on earth don't represent one billionth of our existence. If God's Word makes anything clear, it's the fact that life doesn't end with death. Either heaven and hell are real places or Christianity is the biggest fraud in the history of mankind. How tragic it is to say we *believe* in eternity but spend our lives as if it were a myth.

The fact that this realm of time and space is temporary, yet human life goes on forever, sheds new light on Proverbs 28:19: "He who follows empty pursuits will have poverty in plenty." God is saying that the rich man who neglects the spiritual dimension is bankrupt when it comes to lasting values. Possessions in the here and now cannot influence our eternal destiny, for "riches are not forever" (27:24). When Jesus reenters the earth's atmosphere, and this phase of our existence comes to a screeching halt, *everybody's* bank account goes back to zero. Perhaps that's what Solomon had in mind when he wrote, "Do not weary yourself to gain wealth, cease from your consideration of it. When you set your eyes on it, it is gone. For wealth certainly makes itself wings, like an eagle that flies toward the heavens" (23:4-5).

The New Testament piggybacks on Proverbs' warning about preoccupation with the temporary. Jesus had balloon-popping words for folks who are too earthly minded to be of any heavenly good: "Do not lay up for yourselves treasures upon earth, where moth and rust destroy, and where thieves break in and steal. But lay up for yourselves treasures in heaven, where neither moth nor rust destroys, and where thieves do not break in or steal; for where your treasure is, there will your heart be also" (Matt. 6:19-21). Anyone who has the kind of heavenly heart Jesus talked about takes Proverbs 3:9 seriously: "Honor the Lord from your wealth." That's another way of saying, "Don't spend it all on yourself. Invest part of it to spread the Christian message and support the work of God in the world."

Monumental Decisions

My main fear in discussing this eternal-versus-temporary investment issue is that you'll get the wrong impression. Whoever believes the Bible outlaws savings accounts and mutual funds is going off the deep end. Yet it *is* essential to keep the communication lines with God open and allow the Holy Spirit to ask us hard questions about our resources — financial and otherwise.

• Is our basic orientation in life aimed at material pursuits or at permanent commodities such as a relationship with Christ and His work in the world?

• Are we demonstrating our love for the Lord by giving a portion of our income to His work in the local church?

• Are we using our time, energies, and talents for the Lord in any way, shape, or form? Or does the pursuit of extra income leave us too exhausted to get involved at the church or with other Christian organizations?

• Do we exercise concern for the eternal destiny of family members and friends by praying for their salvation? By sharing Christ with them?

• Could we use financial windfalls — such as garage sale proceeds or that unexpected inheritance — to help support a summer missions trip planned by members of our church?

Whenever God's Spirit questioned him about stewardship of his resources, R.G. LeTourneau listened intently. He started out as an engineer during the economic depression of the 1930s.

From the start he decided to use money to build God's kingdom, not just his own business. By the time he died decades later, he had gone from living on 90 percent of his income and giving 10 percent to just the opposite. He kept 10 percent and gave 90 percent to churches and mission groups! The 10 percent he kept was still a sizeable fortune. LeTourneau felt that such a financial move was logical in view of the Christian message about heaven and hell. He wanted as many folks as possible to hear the Gospel. He designed and built some of the largest earth moving equipment in the world. Yet his eyes were glued to another realm. LeTourneau realized that a person writes his autobiography in his checkbook. He knew in advance that the hearse which would carry his body to the cemetary *wouldn't be pulling a U-Haul!*

Maxey Jarman, the late founder of the Jarman shoe company, gave millions of dollars to various Christian enterprises. Once, when his business fortune suffered a temporary setback, an associate asked him, "Do you ever think about all the money you've given away?" "Yes," Jarman admitted. "But remember: I didn't lose the money I gave to God. I only lost what I kept!" He understood that we can't take our money to heaven, but we *can* send it on ahead.

The examples of LeTourneau and Jarman are in sharp contrast to another man I heard about. Let's pick up the other fellow's story in a book I wrote a few years ago:

Go to a graveyard outside Lincoln, Kansas, and you'll see an unusual group of gravestones. They were erected by a man named Davis. When you delve into his personal history, you discover that he began working as a lowly hired hand. Over the years, though, by sheer determination and extreme frugality, he amassed a wallet-bulging fortune. You also find out that Mr. Davis' preoccupation with wealth resulted in a neglect of people. Apparently he had few friends. He was even emotionally distant from his wife's family, who felt that she had married beneath her dignity.

Their attitude embittered him. He vowed never to leave his relatives a penny.

When his wife died, Davis hired a sculptor to design an elaborate monument in her memory. The monument consisted of a love seat showing Mr. Davis and his wife sitting together. The result so pleased him that he paid for another showing him kneeling at his wife's grave, placing a wreath on it. That was followed by a third monument— showing his wife kneeling at his future gravesite. His monument-building binge continued until he'd spent more than a quarter of a million dollars!

He was often approached about contributing financial aid to worthwhile projects in the town or church. But he rarely gave to them. Most of his small fortune was invested in gravestones. At 92, Mr. Davis died—a sour-hearted resident of the poor house.

Decades later, as you saunter through the graveyard, you notice an ironic fact: each monument he commissioned is slowly sinking into the Kansas soil, a victim of neglect, vandalism, and time. Inevitably, these temporal objects will follow him into the grave.

We're instinctively repelled by such an eccentric expenditure of time and money. "What a waste!" we're prone to cry. We think of loftier, less selfish pursuits that could have enhanced the lives of countless people.

Yet Mr. Davis' strange investments may still reap dividends—if we let the story of his life serve as a stimulus for evaluating our own lives. When is the last time you evaluated how you are investing your life? Consider these soul-jarring questions:

● What are God's objectives for my life?
● To what extent am I investing my life and God-given resources in eternal, rather than just temporal, matters?
● What "monuments" do I want to leave behind when I die?[4]

Ask God to be your broker. Give Him permission to evaluate your "investment portfolio" and make any necessary changes. That's what John did. He decided to become a full-service Christian in a self-serve world. Yvonne Baker Stock originally reported John's story for the readers of *Discipleship Journal.* As you read his account, let the Holy Spirit question *you.*

Young, single, and working for a major high-tech firm as a research and development engineer, John has all the attributes necessary to live the contemporary, comfortable yuppie lifestyle.

So why is he driving a 1982 Honda and spending his vacations building housing in underdeveloped countries?

When he is making decisions on how to spend his money and how to give away his resources, John doesn't compare himself with American men in his age and economic bracket. He compares himself to his fellow Christians around the world and his scriptural responsibilities to them.

For John, this viewpoint has developed gradually. It began five years ago during a missions emphasis week at his church.

"During that week, I asked one of the participants who was from Nigeria, what we could do to help his church. I asked him to tell me his wildest dream." He was totally surprised when the man told him that what they really needed was help in starting a corner filling station.

This interaction made John realize the importance of everyday economic realities in our spiritual interactions with Christians around the world. "I realized that one of my previous assumptions—that hard work, honesty, and integrity always bring one prosperity—was not a biblical norm, but a cultural one.

"As I studied the Bible, looking at Job and others, I realized that being right before God doesn't necessarily guarantee we'll be wealthy in worldly terms."

John decided that he wanted to live his life in awareness of the rest of the world and that he wanted his giving to involve all of his life, not simply the checks he wrote out to his church and Christian missions.

He started by evaluating his checkbook. "I think lots of people are afraid to look at it as one of the spiritual vital signs," John says. "But our checkbooks reflect the biblical truth that where our money is, there our heart will be."

This evaluation caused John to make changes in several areas.

"I try to live as simply as I can," he says. "I try to eat more simply. I'll often have a rice-and-beans sort of meal, in solidarity with my brothers and sisters around the world."

Rather than taking expensive vacations, he has traveled to Third World countries as a volunteer; for example, working with Habitat for Humanity. In doing this he finds more and more areas of his life being influenced because, "Your needs change when the needs of the world are brought into the big picture."

He has also revamped his shopping and gift giving habits. Having come from a generous family, he loved to give gifts. But when he looked more deeply he realized that he often went shopping not just to get things for others, but to make himself feel better. Knowing he could purchase what he wanted gave him a sense of power.

Though he had the choice to buy things or not, he realized that God asked him to exercise his choices wisely. A letter, a simple card, a donation in the name of a friend, these are the things that have now replaced gifts that he says in the past, "simply gathered dust."

"Giving reflects my inward spirit," says John. "It is a struggle with God. How do I define myself: as an American and a consumer, or as a child of God? And if I define myself as a child of God, my happiness is God's responsibility and not mine to manipulate out of life."[5]

To delve deeper into the issue of money management from a biblical perspective, pick up a copy of Larry Burkett's *The Complete Financial Guide For Young Couples* (Victor Books). Larry covers all the financial issues with which couples should be grappling: short-range and long-range goals, insurance, budgets, retirement, investing, giving, and proper financial training for children. He affirms the truths you've gleaned from Proverbs and offers concrete advice for applying them to your life.

Perhaps the best summary of what Proverbs teaches about money is couched in the following words, attributed to C.S. Lewis: "All that is not eternal is eternally useless."

CHAPTER ELEVEN
Treasure Hunt

Not everyone takes advantage of life-enriching resources within his grasp. Tom, from a small town in Massachusetts, is a case in point.

In December 1986, he bought a lottery ticket at a local variety store. Without informing his wife of the purchase, he laid the ticket inside a kitchen cabinet. When the drawing for the $5.8 million jackpot occurred, two winning numbers were announced. But only one winner came forward. In an effort to locate the missing winner, officials announced that the other ticket—worth $2.9 million—was sold at the same variety store Tom used. Since no one else had claimed the prize, odds are that Tom's ticket had the winning digits.

When he found out where the missing winner had purchased a ticket, Tom dashed home faster than a track star on steroids. A couple of hours earlier, though, the ticket had been escorted to the dump with the rest of the trash! Tom's wife had thrown away the priceless piece of paper without realizing its value.

Neither Tom nor his wife slept well that night. He and a gang of friends spent the next two days raking through mounds of trash at the dump in an attempt to find the bag containing his ticket. But they came up empty-handed.[1]

Though it's against my convictions to purchase a lottery ticket, I feel sorry for Tom. A treasure was his to claim, but he treated the ticket too flippantly. The doorway to riches was only an arm's length away, yet he failed to open it. If only. . . .

Tom's experience reminds me of an unfortunate situation in the spiritual realm. Many Christians treat their ticket to spiritual valuables nonchalantly. There is a wealth of wisdom stored in the vault of God's Word, but do we regularly make withdrawals?

I like money as well as the next guy. Yet neglecting an *eternal* treasure such as the Bible is far more tragic than losing a winning lottery ticket.

Why don't folks consult the Bible more often? One reason is a lack of know-how. When we try to read the Bible without a simple, structured procedure, its contents may come across as dully as the fiftieth rerun of a chewing gum commercial. Knowing how to approach the text increases the likelihood of hitting the jackpot.

Reading Proverbs on your own is better for your spiritual health than digesting what any human author has to say about it. That's why I want to wrap up this book by equipping you to make your own discoveries. To conclude chapter 1, I recommended that you read a chapter a day, corresponding to the day of the month. If it's October 12, read Proverbs 12, and so on. The next month, repeat the same procedure. Now it's time to describe a method for exploring each chapter. The approach I'll explain will enable you to hear directly from God Himself! Richard Warren agrees that self-discovery from Scripture is tastier than munching on second-hand insights:

> If I were to meet a starving man by the side of the river, lake, or ocean, I could do one of two things: I could get my fishing rod and catch him a fish, or I could teach him how to fish, thus satisfying his hunger for a lifetime. The second option is obviously the best way to help that man. In the same way, hungry Christians need to be taught how to feed themselves from the Word of God.[2]

Before I explain this method for studying a chapter in Proverbs, though, I'd like to open your mental filters to the following perspectives and tips on Bible study. Methodologies are useless unless we're motivated to practice them.

Hunting Instructions

These observations can improve your chances of striking it rich in the book of Proverbs:

1. *Realize that God wants to spend time with you!* Don't read the Bible to fulfill a religious requirement or to ease pangs of guilt. Read it because it's a means of deepening your relationship with the Lord. Sure, you need the nourishment of God's Word to strengthen you for daily living. You can't stick to your convictions or make an impact for God without a steady diet of spiritual food. Yet more important than the benefits *you* receive is what your devotional time means to the Lord. As your Heavenly Father, He enjoys one-on-one encounters with you. The fact that He desires to spend time with you should prompt you to pray and to read His Word.

In a best-selling booklet about the Christian life, *My Heart — Christ's Home*, Robert Munger tells how this perspective revolutionized his attitude toward Bible study and prayer. The excerpt begins with an imaginary conversation between Jesus and Munger. Jesus is speaking in regard to the author's tendency as a young adult to neglect his devotional life:

"The trouble is that you have been thinking of the quiet time, of Bible study and prayer, as a means for your own spiritual growth. This is true, but you have forgotten that this hour means something to me also. Remember, I love you. At a great cost I have redeemed you. I value your fellowship. Just to have you look up into my face warms my heart. Don't neglect this hour if only for my sake. Whether or not you want to be with me, remember I want to be with you. I really love you!"

You know, the truth that Christ wants my fellowship,

that He loves me, wants me to be with Him, and waits for me, has done more to transform my quiet time with God than any other single fact.[3]

2. *Set realistic goals for your Bible reading.* To resolve to spend an hour a day alone with the Lord is a noble objective. But is it achievable? If you've been neglecting prayer and Bible reading, to go from 0 to 60 minutes overnight calls for a major overhaul in your schedule. Think of it this way: if you set a lofty devotional goal of 60 minutes and you stop after 20, then you're a failure—at least when evaluated by the standard you set! You may feel deflated because you fell short of prior expectations. Yet the truth is, twenty minutes a day may represent a big improvement over your past efforts! Setting goals too high merely saps your motivation.

I know someone who started a "9:59" Bible reading club. He committed himself to read God's Word for 9 minutes and 59 seconds a day. His success at squeezing this smaller chunk of time from his busy schedule gave him an appetite for more. Before you knew it, he was up to 19:59 a day! If we take small steps instead of long strides, changes in our daily routine are more apt to stick.

3. *Cultivate a willingness to work hard.* Even when your reading takes only a few minutes, hitting the jackpot requires focused attention on the text. To skim a chapter with your eyelids at half-mast, or while the kids watch "The Cosby Show" in the background, is a waste of time. You'll need discipline because spine-tingling moments of ecstacy during Bible study are the exceptions rather than the rule.

Youth for Christ worker, Gary Dausey also emphasizes that the hard work of Bible reading takes the form of observing details of the text:

An old Indian asked a stranger if he had seen the man who had stolen his guns. The Indian went on to say that the man was young, short, heavy, and spoke with an Eastern accent. The stranger said, "You must have gotten a good look at him."

"No," was the Indian's reply. "I knew he was young because his footprints in the snow were crisp and showed no signs of dragging feet. He was short because he stood on a box to get to the guns. He was heavy because his footprints sank deep into the snow. He had an Eastern accent because he wore shoes and not cowboy boots."

The Indian knew what to look for—and so can you when it comes to reading God's Word.[4]

The method you'll encounter later on will tell you what to look for in Proverbs. It will serve as a map to help you find spiritual treasures. You'll learn to investigate a chapter with the precision of a Private Eye. As you work at Bible study though, expect to go through at least three stages in your attitude. Howard Hendricks was the speaker who defined these stages for me:

• the *"castor oil"* stage: You study the Bible because you know it's good for you, but it isn't too enjoyable.

• the *"cereal"* stage: Your Bible reading is dry and uninteresting, yet you realize it's nourishing.

• the *"peaches and cream"* stage: You begin enjoying the taste of God's Word.

4. *Set a definite time of day for your Bible reading.* Set your alarm 15 minutes earlier each morning. Or reserve the last few minutes before bedtime. The time of day isn't necessarily important, but committing yourself to a set time increases the likelihood of consistency.

Some of us are zombies before 9:00 A.M. but perky at 11:00 P.M. Don't think you get extra credit with God if you read your Bible before breakfast. It all depends on how God put you together. A lady who has her time alone with God at night said, "If the Lord had intended for me to get up with the sunrise, He would have scheduled it later in the day!"

5. *To keep your rendezvous with God fresh, occasionally read a chapter from two or three different translations.* Start with a paraphrase such as *The Living Bible,* then mull over the same chapter from a literal translation such as *The New International Version* (NIV). Prayerfully look at the text through different lenses, and you won't just *own* a Living Bible—you'll *be* one! After all, the best Bible translation is when we translate what we read into daily experience.

Now it's time to get acquainted with the chapter study method I referred to earlier.

Character Under Construction

Over the years, I've read Proverbs hundreds of times. Recently I asked the Lord for a simple but systematic way to help others claim its treasure. The result is a nine-step method for exploring each chapter of Proverbs. Each step in the process is actually a *cue*—a signal for you to look for a particular topic, or a specific type of content. This approach is based on the "you're-more-apt-to-find-something-if-you're-looking-for-it" principle. It serves the same purpose as a metal detector: the method helps you locate treasure that's buried beneath the surface of the biblical text. I'll explain each step, and illustrate the process from my reading in Proverbs 15.

Communicate. Start your devotional time by *communicating with the Lord.* Ask Him to increase your powers of observation, to show you how verses in the chapter relate to your life. Make King David's prayer your own: "Open my eyes, that I may behold wonderful things from Thy law" (Ps. 119:18). When you finish praying, read the chapter from start to finish. Then shuttle your mind to the next step.

Home. No matter how you rate your family life, an important context for applying Bible truths is the home. As you read a chapter, try to link its content to situations around the house. Does a verse make you think of your relationship with your spouse? With a son or daughter? Does a verse either commend or reprove you about your behavior around the house? A sensitive person could make a connection between almost every verse, and his home life. So to keep you from getting bogged down, on any given day just look for one verse or insight that's relevant to this area of your life. Then proceed to the next step.

As I read Proverbs 15, I pondered this question: *Which verse or truth speaks loudest to things I'm currently experiencing at home?* God's Spirit directed my attention to verse 1: "A gentle answer turns away wrath, but a harsh word stirs up anger." I recalled a recent incident when I reprimanded my two sons for arguing. I corrected them with harsh words of my own. What an example! I yelled at them for yelling at each other! Because I was thinking in terms of a family context, I quickly saw a connection between the verse and my experience. The verse nudged me to confess to the Lord, and to apologize to the boys.

Attitudes. An attitude is the feeling or internal reaction we have toward a person or circumstance. Terms like *hateful, humble, joyous, teachable, pessimistic,* and *thankful* describe attitudes. As you read each chapter in Proverbs, seek answers to these questions: *What attitudes is the Lord complimenting? What attitudes does He censure?* Then bridge the gap from the printed page to your life *by pinpointing one attitude to either cultivate or discard.*

This cue made me sensitive to Proverbs 15:31: "He whose ear listens to life-giving reproof will dwell among the wise." That verse exalts a teachable spirit, a willingness to learn from others' input. The Lord reminded me of how valuable critics are to my ministries of teaching and writing. He doesn't ask me to agree with every critic, but He does expect me to listen. The day I stop learning from others is the day my effectiveness starts to wane.

Relationships. What connections do you see between chapter content and relationships outside the home? Employees, neighbors, work associates, and even cold-blooded enemies are potential targets for your transfer of God's Word into life. Does a verse cause you to evaluate the effect a business companion is having on your attitudes or values? Does a line of copy prick your conscience and remind you to apologize for a comment you made? Does a statement increase your appreciation for a particular friend? The gamut of possibilities seems endless. But once again, keep things simple by finding just one application, then moving to the next phase.

When I viewed Proverbs 15 through the lens of "relationships," my eyes stopped at verse 22: "Without consultation, plans are frustrated, but with many counselors they succeed." I had been wrestling with a decision for days, but couldn't sort through the issues to my satisfaction. The verse reproved me for my solo effort and prodded me to make an appointment with a close friend. His input clarified my alternatives and removed the static from my brain.

Actions. Numerous one-liners in Proverbs refer to deeds or behavior patterns which God either applauds or denounces. In each chapter, try to pinpoint one behavior that God wants you to either curb or implement. James urged his readers to "prove yourselves doers of the Word, and not merely hearers" (James 1:22).

By now you realize that these nine steps aren't mutually exclusive. One of the other cues might also prod you to action. That's okay. Yet it's possible that the word *action* will make you aware of a need that none of the other steps discloses. But heed this warning: don't compile a long list of action plans from each chapter. Trying to obey lots of things at once will overload your circuits and cause frustration.

The *Home* phase of the study convicted me about a harsh tone of voice I had used with my boys. A few minutes later, as I meditated on the chapter in light of the *actions* concept, God's Spirit reminded me again to apologize to my kids later in the day. Two different observation cues worked in tandem to goad me into action. I didn't feel obligated to think of a separate action plan before shifting to the next phase of the study.

Consequences. It's common for a proverb to mention either *negative consequences* or *positive results* of a specific attitude or course of action. If you're looking for such references, you're e apt to hear God's voice whisper a personal word to you. What you read may serve as a restraint to some attitudes or behaviors or an incentive to develop others.

Here's a verse that warned me about the damaging consequences of pride: "The Lord will tear down the house of the proud" (15:25). That remark reminded me of a verse I had memorized from another chapter in Proverbs: "Pride goes before destruction, and a haughty spirit before stumbling" (16:18). The reference to pride reminded me to thank the Lord once again for the success of a recent seminar I had led. When I accept the credit which *He* deserves, the seed of pride has a fertile soil in which to grow.

Tell. Pick one truth or verse from the chapter to pass along to someone else. Did a remark encourage you? Could someone you know receive the same benefit if you shared it? Did God's Spirit expose a problem that you need to share with a friend for the purpose of prayer support? Ask the Lord for an appropriate moment during the day to tell what you learned: over the phone, in a conversation at work, or even in a letter. The Lord doesn't bless or teach us solely for our own benefit.

The Dead Sea is a lake occupying the southern end of the Jordan River Valley. Its northern tip rests near the city of Jerusalem. This sheet of greenish, salty water is 11 miles across at its widest point, and almost 50 miles long. The water itself is marked by a distinctively bitter taste, and a nauseous smell. Do you know why it's called the "Dead" Sea? The water contains so many minerals such as bromide and sulphur that few living things can survive in it. The water houses these minerals and can't support many life forms like a normal lake for one basic reason: *the Dead Sea has inlets, but no outlets.* Millions of tons of water—from the Jordan and several smaller streams—flow into the basin daily. But no streams flow from it to other parts of the country. This salty sea would be fresh or only mildly saline had it an outlet: but the landlocked basin in which it rests in that hot and arid climate serves as a gigantic evaporating pan. Flooding is prevented because the dry heat rapidly evaporates the water.

This fact about the Dead Sea reflects a truth of Christian living: we need to construct outlets so that whatever blessings flow into our lives eventually refresh others as well. Our lives aren't as fresh, reproductive, and attractive if what we're learning and experiencing isn't channeled toward others with whom we have contact.

A college student I teach maintains a cheery disposition even when she's mired in the quicksand of academic pressures. You can tell that her smile wasn't purchased during a blue-light special at K-Mart. It's genuine. After reading Proverbs 15, I complimented her capacity for joy which doesn't seem to fluctuate with the circumstances. Then I quoted the first half of verse 13: "A joyful heart makes a cheerful face."

Entreat. Entreat is a verb that means to ask or plead. You launch your study time by asking the Lord to show you relevant truths. Now you wrap it up by asking Him to help you carry out the action plan you've identified, cultivate or discard an attitude unveiled by the chapter, or transform a relationship you're concerned about. This prayer acknowledges that fleshing out Bible truth is an unnatural phenomenon requiring *supernatural* aid. Even a spiritual Hercules like the Apostle Paul relied on Christ's power rather than his own: "I can do all things *through Him who strengthens me* (Phil. 4:13, emphasis mine). This term can also prod you to probe the chapter in light of this question: "How should what I'm reading affect my prayer life?"

Remember. Which maxim from the chapter impressed you most or leaves the biggest dent on your conscience? Store that verse in your memory bank. A likely choice for memorization is one of the verses you've already identified in the chapter. Memorizing a verse gives the Holy Spirit fuel to work with throughout the day and increases the likelihood of application. King David recognized the practical value of memorizing Scripture: "Thy Word I have treasured in my heart, that I may not sin against Thee" (Ps. 119:11).

Since the Lord had used Proverbs 15:1 to convict me of a rude tone of voice around the house, that's the verse I selected.

Now when I'm tempted to overact during a clash, these words automatically surface on the screen of my mind: "A gentle answer turns away wrath, but a harsh word stirs up anger." The memorized words spur me to whisper an S.O.S. prayer and keep me from a major blow-up.

There's an easy way to remember the series of study steps I've explained. The first letters of each word form an acrostic: **C-H-A-R-A-C-T-E-R**. Exercise this chapter method throughout Proverbs, and God will beef up *your* character. What Paul said about the Bible in general rings true of Proverbs in particular: "All Scripture is inspired by God and profitable for teaching, for reproof, for correction, for training in righteousness" (2 Tim. 3:16).

What follows is a layout of the **CHARACTER** method on paper. Where appropriate, jot down brief insights in the spaces provided. You're free to copy this form or type your own version of it, then make multiple copies for future use. Don't feel obligated to think of a response to *every* cue every single day. It's a tool to enhance your vision as you read—not a mental straitjacket which keeps your creativity under wraps.

Remember Tom, the fellow whose winning lottery ticket wound up at the town dump? How are *you* treating *your* ticket to God's bounty? Try this **CHARACTER** method for a month, and you'll find treasure instead of trash.

CHARACTER Chapter Study Method

Communication	Before you read, ask the Lord to help you see and understand things in the text.
Home	Which verse or truth speaks most clearly to what I'm currently experiencing at home? Explain.
Attitudes	What attitude referred to in the chapter should I cultivate or discard?
Relationships	Does a verse or truth from the chapter suggest an application to any of my relationships outside the home? Explain.
Actions	What deed/behavior pattern referred to in the chapter should I either adopt or curb?

CHARACTER Chapter Study Method

Consequences	What positive or negative consequences of some specific activity/attitude does God want to impress on me? Why?
Tell	The verse or truth that God wants me to pass along to someone else is . . . The individual or group with whom I could share this is . . .
Entreat	Ask the Lord to help you follow through on one or more application ideas identified so far.
Remember	Write out the verse and reference from this chapter that would be most helpful for you to memorize.

CHAPTER TWELVE
The Value of Knowing the Scoop

Several years ago I received a harsh letter from a lawyer, informing me that a woman was suing me over an auto accident that
had occurred a year earlier. The suit asked for a jury trial,
$30,000 in remuneration, *plus* "punitive" damages the amount
of which would be decided by the court. Since my liability
insurance covered up to $25,000, there was an outside possibili-
ty of losing big bucks. I bit my fingernails to the quick at the
prospect.

Though my improper turn completely demolished her Buick,
the woman seemed physically fit at the scene of the accident.
The insurance company representative confirmed my suspicions
and said she was trying to rip me off. When my insurer refused
to pay her exaggerated monetary claims, she hired a lawyer and
filed the suit. That's when the insurer hired its own lawyer, and
a series of phone calls and letters seeking accident information
was routed.

Over a nine-month period, I heard several horror stories
about individuals who were victims of unethical lawsuits, yet
who lost their court cases. One fellow wound up losing his
business and his house over a suit that seemingly had no chance

of winning. Occasionally I'd lay awake at night, worrying about the status of the lawsuit, wondering if a jury would fall for her fraudulent injury claims.

Finally, I phoned the insurance company to see why the process was taking so long, and if a court date had been scheduled. I discovered that the suit had been settled out of court *six months earlier!* The insurance company had forgotten to inform me of the fact. The amount she received was well under the $25,000 liability coverage.

Imagine . . . a fact I wasn't aware of negatively affected the quality of my life over a six-month period. Had I known the suit was settled and I was in no danger of losing money, I would have slept better and worried less. Musing on that experience, I discovered the hard way that *what you don't know can hurt you.* Keeping informed definitely pays dividends.

That's true in the spiritual realm, too. *When we're uninformed concerning doctrines and principles of living couched in the Bible, what we don't know can stunt our spiritual growth and usefulness to God.* This paperback is chock-full of helpful knowledge from Proverbs, but it certainly doesn't exhaust what God wants you to know from this practical section of His Word.

The following pages offer you an opportunity to increase your knowledge of God's perspectives on timely issues. Rather than *telling* you what Proverbs says on fresh topics, I'll try to whet your appetite for your own discovery in Scripture. You'll read an introduction to four new subjects addressed in Proverbs, encounter a list of passages addressing those subjects, then discover a series of questions you can answer by studying those verses on your own.

Sow the following biblical truths into the fertile soil of your mind and watch a more virile faith sprout up.

Who's Afraid of God?
In a captivating column titled "Why Don't Sinners Cry Anymore?" Joe Bayly lamented the absence of brokenness and tears in our relationship with God:

British thinker-preacher Martyn Lloyd-Jones once com-
mented that people no longer weep at evangelistic meetings. They laugh, he said, they come happily to the front,
but they don't mourn over their sins. . . .

Godly sorrow for sin that leads to repentance is almost
totally absent from our preaching and from our lives. The
one who enters the kingdom without repentance hardly
finds need for it as a resident. We have lost the ability to
say "I'm sorry" to God and to one another. We have lost it
as persons and we have lost it in our churches and we have
lost it as a nation. . . .

Joseph C. Macaulay told of a visit to the Herbrides Is-
lands some years ago, when revival was going on. On his
way to church, where he was to preach, Dr. Macaulay
heard a man sobbing in a cottage as he passed.

"What's that?" he asked his companion.

"That's John. He's on his way to God. He'll come
through," was the reply.[1]

Bayly's words are more relevant today than when he originally
penned them. We seldom mourn sin's presence in our lives
because we have such a dim view of God's majesty and holiness.
Proverbs suggests a remedy: *a restoration of the fear of God.*

Perhaps we've emphasized God's compassion and forgiveness
to the exclusion of His distaste for sin and call for righteousness.
For every person who holds an *unhealthy* fear of God and fails to
appropriate His forgiveness, there are hundreds who treat sin
and its effect on God too flippantly. The longer I study Scripture
the clearer it becomes: God's love for us isn't weak or sentimen-
tal. Taking His grace for granted and treating disobedience casu-
ally is an invitation for Him to discipline us. Proverbs hammers
this point deeply into our consciousness: *a "fear of God" is
commended and expected among His followers.* Fear of men makes
me a coward; fear of God makes me a hero.

Crack open your Bible and graze on the following references
to a "fear of the Lord":

Proverbs 1:7, 29   10:27   22:4
         2:5   14:2, 26-27   23:17
         3:7   15:16, 33   24:21
         8:13   16:6   28:14
         9:10   19:23   31:30

● Based on your analysis of these verses, how would you define a "fear of the Lord"?

● What words/phrases from the verses refer to benefits or rewards of fearing God?

● What is the effect of a healthy fear of God on human behavior? On our attitude toward sin?

● What is the relationship between a healthy fear of the Lord and enticements to sin?

● What relationship can you find between a fear of the Lord and humility?

● How do the following references add to or reinforce Proverbs' teaching on this subject?

    Exodus 20:20   Psalm 34:9
    Deut. 10:12   Psalm 90:11
    Job 37:22-24   Psalm 145:19
    Psalm 31:19   Isaiah 6:1-5

● What painful consequences of sin experienced by believers I know should create a "fear of God" in my heart and serve as a deterrent to my own sin?

The Winsome Worker

In *Living Beyond the Daily Grind, Book II,* Charles Swindoll tells about a young fellow who rushed into a gas station to use the pay phone. The station manager overheard the telephone conversation as the young man asked:

"Sir, could you use a hardworking, honest young man to work for you?" (Pause) "Oh . . . you've already got a hardworking, honest young man? Well, thanks anyway!"

The boy hung up the phone with a smile. Humming to himself, he began to walk away, obviously happy.

"How can you be so cheery?" asked the eavesdropping service station manager. "I thought the man you talked to already had someone and didn't want to hire you."

The young fellow answered, "Well, you see I *am* the hardworking young man. I was just checking up on my job!"[2]

Then Swindoll piggybacked on the anecdote, and posed the following question to his readers: "If you called your boss, disguised your voice, and asked about *your* job, what do you think would be the boss' answer?"

The caller obviously demonstrated *diligence* on the job—an observable and impressive trait in the eyes of his supervisor. Proverbs is teeming with references to diligence and work-related attitudes. God feels that this particular quality should be taken off the endangered species list and cultivated into our character.

Snap on your zoom lens and focus on Proverbs' references to either *diligence* or *laziness*. (Remember: a thorough topical analysis requires a look at *antonyms*—words with opposite meanings—as well an *synonyms*.) Keys words include *diligence, work, slothful, sluggard,* and *lazy*. Examine the Scripture references, then mull over the questions. Even when a key term isn't employed, the *concept* is addressed in each passage.

Proverbs	6:6-11	16:3, 26	24:30-34
	10:4-5, 26	18:9	26:14-16
	12:11, 24, 27	19:15, 24	30:24-25
	13:4, 11	20:4, 13	31:10-31
	14:4, 23	21:5, 25-26	
	15:19	22:29	

• What words/phrases from these verses show the positive consequences of diligence? The negative consequences of laziness?

• According to these verses, what are some specific ways in which diligence shows in a person? How does a lack of diligence show?

● Which reference implies that slothfulness results in a negative testimony among people we know?

● Which verse implies that diligence is a trait we should objectively evaluate before serving as an employment reference for another person?

● How is diligence—or the absence of it—linked to the concept of "planning ahead"?

● Which verses encourage us to share, rather than to hoard, any material rewards of diligence?

X-rated Christians

J. Allan Petersen wrote a timely book titled *The Myth of the Greener Grass*. He speaks frankly about extramarital affairs and offers both preventive and healing measures. To start the book, he shares a story which demonstrates the moral erosion occurring in far too many believers:

"How come you didn't finish the story?" he asked, shaking my hand as he left the late-morning session at the conference for men. I had told the story of a man whose unfaithfulness had ruined his own marriage, caused a divorce in another family, and left indelible scars on his children.

"What do you mean?" I inquired.

"Petersen, that story doesn't usually end in tragedy and disappointment; it's often through an extramarital affair that a person finds true love, happiness, and joy for the first time. Can we have lunch together?"

In the car, driving to the restaurant, I learned that this plain-looking middle-aged man was a minister, pastoring three small churches in the area. Although married to a beautiful and talented woman (his own description), he was deeply involved with a young pianist in one of his churches.

"My wife is a good woman, but when I married her, it was only an intellectual decision, and we didn't know what love was. Our marriage is solid, but not too exciting, and our three teen-aged children are getting along fine."

"Tell me about the pianist."

"I started making pastoral calls at her home when her children were at school and her husband was at work. I discovered we were compatible in so many ways, and there was an aliveness about her that my wife didn't have. I liked the way I acted and felt when I was with her. The first time we had sex together it was out of this world." With nervous excitement in his voice, he continued, "She is so uninhibited and fulfills every sexual fantasy I ever had. I hadn't ever had much fun in my life; I had never felt young, romantic, or sexy. For the first time I've discovered what real love is all about. We have a right to be happy, don't we? Anything this good has to be right. I would rather go to hell with her than to heaven with my wife."

"Real love?" I asked.

"Certainly! I am always looking out for her best interests. I would never hurt her. I wouldn't think of having intercourse with her while she was having her period or when she would be apt to get pregnant."

"If this is true love, why don't you divorce your wife and marry her?" I suggested, facetiously.

"What? You must be kidding! Why, that would be wrong. I don't want to hurt my wife and break up two families."[3]

Sexual sin is another subject that frequently crops up in the Book of Proverbs. If you're serious about maintaining marital fidelity, tuck the following passages into the creases of your mind, then mull over the accompanying questions. What God says can serve as an antidote to the "X-rated Christian" syndrome.

Proverbs	2:16-19	7:4-27	23:26-28
	4:23	9:13-18	29:3
	5:3-23	14:14	30:20
	6:23-35	22:3	31:3

● Which references offer "preventive strategies" for staying sexually pure? What are those strategies?

● What concrete forms can "watch over your heart with all diligence" take? (4:23) What practical forms can "hiding one's self from evil" take? (22:3)

● What arguments for sexual purity do the various references contain?

● What words/phrases from these passages refer to the painful consequences of sexual indulgence?

The Peril of Pride

Have you ever witnessed the execution of a frog? A few folks have—back in a high school or college chemistry class. The teacher puts the unsuspecting creature in a large beaker of cool water. Then he scoots a Bunsen burner beneath the beaker and ignites a very low flame. That small flame heats the water very slowly—several hundredths of a degree per second—so the water temperature escalates gradually. Class members check the beaker a couple of hours later, and they find a dead frog. He has boiled to death!

Here's the surprising part. Anyone who keeps his eyes glued to the frog the whole time never sees the creature squirm or try to jump out of the water. The change occurs so slowly that the frog is never aware of it. He never realizes that he's in any danger.

Every time I recall that gruesome demonstration, I think of how gradually a person's attitudes and values can erode. Sin rarely destroys a person's life instantaneously. Rather, the change happens subtly, over a period of time. If we're not careful, we suddenly find ourselves in boiling water with no avenue of escape.

What ignites the process of moral erosion in people? What is it that plops a person into the water and causes the temperature to rise in the first place? There's more than *one* answer to those questions. Yet God's Word suggests that one attitude, above all others, serves as a catalyst for deterioration of character. When this particular flame flickers in the heart, an erosive process is inevitable.

The flame I have in mind is *pride.*

Take what Proverbs says about pride to heart, and you'll save yourself from a lot of hot water. By the time you finish your investigation of this subject, you'll understand why Amy Carmichael wrote, "Those who think too much of themselves don't think enough!"

Following the tracks of *pride* through Proverbs requires keeping an eye out for terms such as *arrogant, haughty, boasting, humble,* as well as *pride* or *proud.* If you put the following references under your mental microscope, you should find answers to the related study questions.

Proverbs		
3:5-7	16:5, 18-19	26:12
6:3, 17	18:12	27:1-2, 21
8:13	21:4, 24	28:25-26
11:2	22:4	29:23
15:25, 33	25:6-7, 14, 27	30:8-9, 13, 32

● What effect does pride have on our relationships?

● In what ways does pride show up in a person? (What attitudes and actions indicate that pride has nuzzled its way into the heart?)

● What words/phrases from these verses show that a proud person eventually reaps negative consequences?

● What phrases from the biblical texts show how God feels about pride? Why is pride so distasteful to the Lord?

● According to Proverbs 27:21 and 30:8-9, what factors can give birth to a proud spirit?

● What is the relationship between pride, and a presumptuous attitude toward the future? (See Proverbs 27:1, as well as James 4:13-16.)

● For a case study which vividly illustrates what Proverbs teaches on pride, read the account of King Uzziah in 2 Chronicles 26. Which specific verses or truths from Proverbs were demonstrated by Uzziah's experience?

Remember the lawsuit referred to in the introduction to this chapter? The absence of factual information diminished the quality of my life for a six-month period. I didn't know that a person in authority—a judge— had ruled in my favor and provided anxiety-reducing information.

Don't let a lack of biblical information cripple your Christian walk. The ultimate authority figure has spoken on a variety of issues relevant to daily living. What you don't know about these topics can adversely affect you. Delve into Proverbs on your own, and even if *you* are slapped with a lawsuit, you'll be able to view the situation from God's perspective.

NOTES

Chapter 1: Gaining God's Perspective

1. Charles Swindoll, *Growing Strong in the Seasons of Life* (Portland, Ore.: Multnomah Press, 1983), p. 71.

2. Fred Smith, *You and Your Network* (Waco, Texas: Word Books, 1984), p. 98.

3. Calvin Miller, *The Taste of Joy* (Downers Grove, Ill.: InterVarsity Press, 1983), p. 23.

4. Haydn L. Gilmore, "Biblical Proverbs: God's Transistorized Wisdom," *Christianity Today* (Aug. 19, 1966), pp. 6–8.

5. Charles Sell, *The House on the Rock* (Wheaton, Ill.: Victor Books, 1988), pp. 14–15).

6. Ibid., p. 15.

7. Ibid., pp. 19–20.

Chapter 2: Finishing What We Start

1. "Anthony Munoz Blocks *Playboy* at the Line of Scrimmage," *Focus on the Family* (May 1987), p. 10.

2. Chris Zwingelberg, "Sin's Peril," *Leadership* (Winter 1987), p. 41.

3. David Morley, "Sex Under Control," *HIS* (Nov. 1971), pp. 6–7.

4. Erwin Lutzer, *Living with Your Passions* (Wheaton, Ill.: Victor Books, 1983), pp. 116–117.

5. Charles Swindoll, *Living on the Ragged Edge* (Waco, Texas: Word Books, 1985), p. 48.

Chapter 3: Open Mouth, Insert Foot

1. "Talk Isn't Cheap at WSCQ Radio," *The State*, Columbia, S.C.

2. Loren Caroll, *Conversation, Please.*

3. Terry Powell, "How to Lie Without Really Trying," *Free-Way* (Spring 1973), p. 2.

4. Carole Mayhall, *Words That Hurt, Words That Heal* (Colorado Springs, Colo.: NavPress, 1986), p. 54.

5. *USA Today*, June 20, 1989.

6. Charles Swindoll, *Growing Strong in the Seasons of Life* (Portland, Ore.: Multnomah Press, 1983), p. 21.

7. Warren Wiersbe, *Be Mature* (Wheaton, Ill.: Victor Books, 1978), p. 99.

Chapter 4: Conversation Under Construction

1. Herman Helms, *The State*, Columbia, S.C. (March 27, 1988), Sports Section, p. 1.

2. Virgil Vogt, "The Encouragement Connection," *New Covenant.*

3. *The State*, Columbia, S.C.

Chapter 5: How to Make Wise Choices

1. James Dobson, *Focus on the Family* (Feb. 24, 1986), p. 2.

2. Terry Powell, "Trust You with My Life?" *Radiant Tidings Magazine* (Summer 1973), p. 4.

3. Mark Mayfield, "Kids Fret Yet Don't Save for College," *USA Today* (June 18, 1989), p. 10.

4. Paul Lee Tan, *Encyclopedia of 7,700 Illustrations* (Rockville, Md.: Assurance Publishers, 1979), p. 1371.

Chapter 6: Cultivating Our Response-Ability

1. Greg Walter and Andrea Fine, "His Wife Tried (More Than Once) to Kill Him, but Tony Toto Is Alive, Well—and Phoning Her in Prison," *People Weekly* (May 7, 1984), pp. 88–90.

2. Barbara Varenhorst, *Real Friends: Becoming the Friend You'd Like to Have* (San Francisco, Calif.: Harper & Row, 1984), p. 58.

3. Irene and Merton Strommen, *Five Cries of Parents* (San Francisco, Calif.: Harper & Row, 1985), pp. 60–62. Used by permission.

4. Charles Swindoll, *Living Beyond the Daily Grind, Book II* (Waco, Texas: Word Books, 1988), p. 438.

Chapter 7: How to Handle a Critic

1. Charles Swindoll, *Living Above the Level of Mediocrity* (Waco, Texas: Word Books, 1987), pp. 126–127.

2. Gordon MacDonald, *Restoring Your Spiritual Passion* (Nashville, Tenn.: Oliver-Nelson, 1986), pp. 189–191.

3. Jeanne Wright, "The All New Jessica Hahn," *USA Today* (July 29, 1988), p. 2D.

4. Charles Swindoll, *Living Above the Level of Mediocrity*, p. 133.

5. Gordon MacDonald, *Ordering Your Private World*, Expanded Edition (Nashville, Tenn.: Oliver-Nelson, 1984), p. 106.

6. John Alexander, *Practical Criticism: Giving It and Taking It* (Downers Grove, Ill.: InterVarsity, 1976), p. 30.

Chapter 8: Living With an Executive

1. Tim LaHaye, *Ten Steps to Victory Over Depression* (Grand Rapids: Zondervan Publishing House, 1974).

2. "Macho Ex-Marine Admits Failure As Housewife," Associated Press release.

Chapter 9: Earthly-Minded

1. Charles Swindoll, *Growing Strong in the Seasons of Life* (Portland, Ore.: Multnomah Press, 1983), p. 147.

2. Ibid., p. 147.

3. John MacArthur, "Mastery of Materialism." As quoted by Ron Blue, "Money—If God Owns It All, What Are You Doing With It?" *Discipleship Journal* (Issue 53, 1989), p. 22.

4. Steve Thurman, "Life, Liberty, and the Pursuit of Just a Little More," *Discipleship Journal* (Issue 53, 1989), p. 27.

5. "Passing College Classes for the Buck," *Youthworker Update* (Feb., 1988), p. 1. Originally in *New York Times*, Jan. 14, 1988.

6. "Having More, We Give Less," *Youthworker Update* (Feb., 1989), p. 3.

7. "Financial Insecurity Dominates Americans' Family Worries," *Emerging Trends* (Vol. 9, No. 9, Nov. 1987), p. 3.

8. Thurman, "Life, Liberty, and the Pursuit of Just a Little More," p. 27.

9. Wayne Beissert and Hugh Wright, "Dream Lives: 'I'll Be Rich Tomorrow,' " *USA Today* (April 26, 1989), pp. 1–2D.

10. Thurman, "Life, Liberty, and the Pursuit of Just a Little More," p. 29.

11. George MacDonald, *The Lady's Confession*, edited by Michael Phillips (Minneapolis, Minn.: Bethany House Publishers, 1986), pp. 33–35. Used by permission.

12. George Gallup, Jr., "Secularism and Religion: Trends in Contemporary America," *Emerging Trends* (Vol. 9, No. 10, Dec. 1987), p. 3.

13. Swindoll, *Growing Strong in the Seasons of Life*, p. 271.

Chapter 10: Releasing Your Resources

1. "Economy Is One Thing, But . . ." *The State*, Columbia, S.C. (Feb. 22, 1989), p. 2A.

2. Danny Lehmann, "Rich Religion: The Hundredfold Heresy," brochure from *Last Days Ministries*.

3. Charles Swindoll, *Living Above the Level of Mediocrity* (Waco, Texas: Word Books, 1987), pp. 158-159.

4. Terry Powell, *Welcome to Your Ministry* (Elgin, Ill.: David C. Cook, 1987), pp. 9–10.

5. Yvonne Baker Stock, "John: Living Simply to Give More," *Discipleship Journal* (Issue 53, 1989), pp. 44–45.

Chapter 11: Treasure Hunt

1. "Search for Lottery Ticket Futile," *Columbia Record*, Columbia, S.C. (Dec. 17, 1986).

2. Richard Warren, *Dynamic Bible Study Methods* (Wheaton, Ill.: Victor Books, 1981), pp. 9–10.

3. Robert Munger, *My Heart—Christ's Home* (Downer's Grove, Ill.: InterVarsity, 1986), pp. 11–12.

4. Gary Dausey, "Come Alive" (*Radiant Tidings Magazine*, Summer 1973), pp. 8–9.

Chapter 12: The Value of Knowing the Scoop

1. Joe Bayly, "Why Don't Sinners Cry Anymore?" (*Eternity*, Oct. 1974), pp. 71–72.

2. Charles Swindoll, *Living Beyond the Daily Grind, Book II* (Waco, Texas: Word Books, 1988), p. 415.

3. J. Allan Petersen, *The Myth of the Greener Grass* (Wheaton, Ill.: Tyndale, 1983), pp. 9–10.

A NOTE FROM THE AUTHOR

Letters are a "first class" way to communicate. If I've said anything in this book that you'd like to salute, to shoot down, or to discuss at greater length, drop me a note.

Ministries which God has given me include speaking on Bible themes at churches or conferences and leading teacher-training seminars for church volunteers. To serve your church or organization in this way would be a lofty privilege.

My address is:
Terry Powell
Columbia Bible College
P.O. Box 3122
Columbia, S.C. 29230